Hypnotic Scripts for Clinical Hypnosis Practitioners

Compiled by Kyra Schaefer

Hypnotic Scripts for Clinical Hypnosis Practitioners

Copyright © 2021. All rights reserved. The author is responsible for their individual opinions expressed through their words. The author retains the copyright to their script in this book. No part of this publication may be reproduced, distributed, or transmitted to any form or by any means, including photocopying, recording, or other electronic, mechanical methods, without the prior written permission of the publisher.

As You Wish Publishing, LLC
Connect@asyouwishpublishing.com

ISBN-13: 978-1-951131-28-9

Printed in the United States of America.

Nothing in this book or any affiliations with this book is a substitute for medical or psychological help. If you need help, please seek it.

How to use this book

This book is a collection of scripts designed by clinical hypnotherapist practitioners.

If you have purchased this book, you are likely a clinical hypnotist or studying hypnosis and want to make a difference in your life or the lives of others.

When you set up your session script, be sure to use the scripts in this order:

- Induction
- Deepener
- Script
- Awakening

Some scripts have included all aspects. Others are only scripts and so on. When working with clients, I bookmark my favorite scripts to easily access during the session.

A note about Process/Non-Process. Those who easily go into trance are Non-Process, and those with a more active mind are Process individuals as they need an additional process to allow for the suggestions to become more sticky. I recommend you use a process and then the suggestions while their mind is busy with the focusing on the activity you are asking them to engage with and then the awakening.

You may also notice ellipses (…) between words and sentences. You may also notice some additional grammatical issues. That is the way of the hypnotherapist!

Our minds process information differently when being spoken to. These scripts are designed to be the most effective when read aloud either into a recording device or for a client.

Although you don't need a certification to practice hypnotherapy, it is however very beneficial to get training to deepen your practice for self care and the care of others.

The following scripts are perfect for Clinical Hypnotists to add variety for their clients. You may also discover some of those hard-to-find scripts instead of creating them yourself.

Table of Contents

Relaxing the Whole Body (Induction 1)
By Kyra Schaefer, CHI 1

Process Full Body Relaxation (Induction 2)
By Kyra Schaefer, CHI 3

Non-Process Energy Relaxation (Induction 3)
By Kyra Schaefer, CHI 5

Drawing Clouds (Process 1)
By Kyra Schaefer 7

Counting Beans (Process 2)
By Kyra Schaefer 9

Map of the World (Process 3)
By Kyra Schaefer 11

Sail Boat Deepener (Deepener 1)
By Kyra Schaefer, CHI 13

Steps to the Beach (Deepener 2)
By Kyra Schaefer, CHI 15

Cloud Count (Deepener 3)
By Kyra Schaefer, CHI 17

Forest Steps (Deepener 4)
By Kyra Schaefer, CHI 19

Blowing Leaves (Deepener 5)
By Kyra Schaefer, CHI 21

Stepping Stone Bridge (Non-Process Deepener)
By Carolyn Mackey CHT 23

Abundance
By Jane Nelson, CHT 29

Abundance II
By Steve Haight, CHT 33

The Achiever
By Bethany Orrick, CHT 35

Bedwetting Script By
Kyra Schaefer, CHI 37

Career Change
By Laura Post, CHT 41

Clutter-Free Living
By Shelly Marsh, CHT 43

Clutter Script / Disorganization
By Amanda Martin, CHT 45

Confidence Boost
By Kim Balzan, CHT 47

Diabetes: Type 1 (Insulin-dependent)
By Laura Post, CHT 49

Feeding Horses (Process Vehicle)
By Carolyn Mackey CHT 53

Fear of Dogs
By Todd Schaefer, CHT 57

Finding Purpose
By Bethany Orrick, CHT 59

First Induction, Deepener & Awakening
By W. Randall Dunning, CHT 61

First Time Hypnosis Suggestion Script
By W. Randall Dunning, CHT 67

Gratefulness Script
By Tibbeth Jordan, CHT 71

Healing and Peace During Pregnancy
By Kate Nethercott Wilson, CHT 73

Healing Athletic Injuries
By Freddy Sandoval, CHT 79

Insecurity
By Rita Lake, CHT 81

Loving Yourself
By Andria M. Pacinelli, CHT 83

Low Self-Esteem
By Mary Stoner, CHT 85

Nail Biting
By Jane Nelson, CHT 87

Owning Your Emotions
By Amanda Martin, CHT 89

Professional Baseball Confidence
By Freddy Sandoval, CHT 93

Releasing a Romantic Relationship
By Kyra Schaefer, CHI 95

School Performance
By Andria M. Pacinelli, CHT 99

Self-Confidence
By Karen L Chaney, CHT 103

Self Love, Self Worth
By Shelly Marsh, CHT 105

Feelings of Unworthiness Script
By Garvin De Shazier, CHT 109

Sewing Improvement
By Connie Brown, CHT 113

Smoking Cessation
By Leslie Freidlander, CHT 115

Smoking Cessation II
By Shirley Dunlap, CHT 117

Transition to Motherhood
By Kate Nethercott Wilson, CHT 123

Compulsive Eating While Watching TV Script
By Garvin De Shazier, CHT 129

The Ultimate Goal Achievement Script
By Steve Haight, CHT 133

Weight Loss I
By Mary Stoner, CHT 137

Weight loss II Increased Metabolism
By Leslie Freidlander, CHT 141

Weight Loss III Physical Health
By Karen L Chaney, CHT 143

Weight Loss IV
By Rita Lake, CHT 147

Weight Loss, Reflection
By Tibbeth Jordan, CHT 149

Weight Management
By Shirley Dunlap, CHT 153

Weight Release
By Kim Balzan, CHT 157

Writing a Best Seller
By Connie Brown, CHT 161

Awakening I
By Kyra Schaefer, CHI 163

Awakening II
By Kyra Schaefer, CHI 165

Awakening III
By Kyra Schaefer, CHI 167

Relaxing the Whole Body (Induction 1)
By Kyra Schaefer, CHI

Begin by allowing a relaxing feeling to begin at the top of your head… this relaxing feeling now moves down to your forehead… your eyes… and eyelids…

Allow that feeling of relaxation… to continue down into your jaw… make sure your teeth are not clenched together… relax your neck and your throat… give the weight of your head over to the pillow…

Allow that feeling of relaxation to continue down into your chest… and abdomen… continue to breathe in and out in that way… that helps you feel the most comfortable… the most relaxed…

Relax your upper, middle and lower back… and give the weight of your body over to the chair or the mattress… relax your arms from your shoulders… down to your elbows… all the way to your fingertips…

Allow that feeling of relaxation to continue in your

hips... down through your legs... relax your knees... relax your calves and shins... relaxing your legs all the way... to your ankles and the tips of your toes...

Relaxing peacefully and easily...

Process Full Body Relaxation (Induction 2)
By Kyra Schaefer, CHI

Get into a comfortable position... make yourself as relaxed as you canbe... eliminate all outside noises and sounds...

Begin to think about relaxing your body... think about relaxing the top of your head... and as you think about relaxing the top of your head... begin to think about relaxing your forehead... your eyebrows, and your eyelids...

As you think about relaxing your eyebrows and eyelids... begin to considerhow good it would feel to relax your jaw... as you allow that feeling of relaxation to move into your jaw... allow your throat that feeling of relaxation...

Allow all outside sounds to relax you further... there's no need to give your attention to anything happening outside of your awareness... and outside of your body...

As your throat and neck relax... you relax your shoulders... those shoulders relax easily and effortlessly... as you relax your arms... you may even get a sense... of your hands feeling as though one hand may feel heavier than the other... I don't know which hand feels heaviest and which feels lightest... the right hand or the left hand... but you do... and you relaxthem even more now...

Take a deep breath in... and as you exhale, relax all of your chest muscles and stomach muscles... relax your upper, middle, and lower back... relax your hips... relax your knees... your thighs... your legs... all the way to the tips of your toes.

Allow that feeling of relaxation to flow through your arms and your legs peacefully and easily... just let go... breathing in and out in a way that feels the best to you... this is your time... your space to... completelyrelax...

Non-Process Energy Relaxation (Induction 3)
By Kyra Schaefer, CHI

Get into a comfortable position... know that you can move anytime you need throughout this entire process to help you become more comfortable and relaxed... you needn't feel stuck to your chair... you can just relax peacefully... easily...

Beginning by using your imagination... imagining what peaceful light... starting from the top of your head... going down towards the bottoms of your feet... this beautiful light is any color you would like it to be...

Taking a couple good deep breaths in and exhaling fully... you see and experience and imagine that light... moving down through your head... through your brain... through your eyes... that feeling of peace and rejuvenation moves down through your eyes... your ears... your nose... your mouth... through your jaw... relaxing your jaw completely... that peaceful relaxation continues down through your throat and neck...

That light... that beautiful light continues across

your shoulders down through your arms... and moves out through your fingertips and the palms of your hands... as you relax peacefully and easily... imagining that light going d-o-w-n... d-o-w-n through your chest and abdomen that light moves through all of your organs... through all of your bones... through all of your blood... through your circulatory system... that light moves through your lungs... through your breath...

That beautiful light moves through your upper, middle and lower back... it moves through your hips... d-o-w-n through your legs... down past your knees... past your ankles and out through the bottoms of your feet and the tips of your toes.

You are in a complete and total flow of positive energy... as you peacefully move into a deeper state... of relaxation now...

Drawing Clouds
(Process 1)
By Kyra Schaefer

As you continue to relax, I am going to invite you to use your imagination. Imagine yourself laying down outside on the most relaxing piece of furniture you can. Describe this piece of furniture to yourself. Is it soft and cushy or something else. Just enjoy this process of allowing yourself to discover the most relaxing piece of furniture you can find. Outside, the day is perfect, peaceful and relaxing, the exact right temperature for you. That's right. Now picture the setting. What feels the best, trees, a beach scene or an open meadow. Whatever you prefer. Take a moment and get this all very clear in your mind.

Look up now at the sky, a few clouds drifting by. It's almost as if you could reach out and touch them.

They form shapes of animals and other shapes as the soft breeze blows. As you point up to the sky, you realize that you can move the clouds with your finger. You begin to draw swirls and shapes.

Finding this interesting, you begin to draw numbers. You draw the number 100. You find this begins to relax you further and more deeply than before. Then you draw the number 99. Deeper into relaxation, you drift.

In a moment, I'm going to have you continue to draw the numbers very slowly, all the way down to 1. I will invite you to pay total attention to your task, no longer listening to me. Like a radio playing in the background, I'll be speaking to you, but there is no need for you to listen. I'll be speaking to your powerful subconscious mind. Your subconscious mind is always listening and always paying attention even when you are deeply asleep or wide awake.

Go ahead and begin now. With each number you write, you go more deeply into relaxation. Continue now with number 98 and then 97. Drifting deeper with each number. When you reach the number 1 you can listen to me once again… That's right, good…. (Suggestions)

Counting Beans (Process 2) By Kyra Schaefer

Imagine yourself now sitting comfortably at a large kitchen countertop. Out in front of you is a large pile of 100 different types of uncooked beans.

There are black beans, white beans and red beans. Your task will be to sort these beans by color one at a time. There are 33 black beans, 34 white beans and 33 red beans. There are 3 jars in front of you. You will put one black bean in the first jar, one white bean in the second jar, and 1 red bean in the 3rd jar until all the jars are filled with the beans. Take your time, and with each bean you drop into a jar, you will let yourself feel more relaxed.

Go ahead now and put one black bean in the jar, good, and one white bean in the jar, that's right and one red bean in the jar. Well done.

Taking your time and focusing on your task, hold on one moment before you continue putting beans in the jars. As you are doing this, I will be speaking to your subconscious mind. You will hear me, but I don't want you to pay any attention to me, like a radio playing in the background of your mind. Your subconscious mind is always listening and paying attention.

Simply focus on your task and continue to relax. If your mind strays away from your task, simply bring it back. Ok, continue your task now, placing the second black bean, the second white bean and the second red bean in the jar. When you are complete with the final bean, you can begin listening to me again. That's right, focused on your task, relaxing with each bean you drop into the jar. Calmer and calmer, (Suggestions)

Map of the World (Process 3) By Kyra Schaefer

Allowing yourself to continue relaxing, I am going to invite you to imagine a huge world map in front of you. You can reach out and touch this map. You can see the outline of many countries. On the table next to you, there is a large box of crayons. In a moment, you are going to start filling in the countries' names, starting by finding the country's name that starts with the letter A. You will pick a color crayon from your box and write in the name of that country on the map.

Go ahead and do that now, find that country that starts with the letter A. Write in that name… Good. Now you will find the country that starts with the letter B and write in that name with a different colored crayon. Good, now hold on a moment while I continue to explain your instructions. You will continue to write in all the countries you can find. With each country you find and each name you write, you will become more and more relaxed. As you continue your task, I don't want you to listen to me anymore. Just let yourself focus totally on your task, I will be speaking to you, and you will be hearing me, but let yourself enjoy what you are working on as I will be speaking to your subconscious mind that is always paying attention and always listening.

Continue with the letter C and so on, no longer paying attention to me. When you reach the letter Z, you can begin to listen to me once again. Allowing each country you write to take you deeper into relaxation. That'sright… (Suggestions)

Sail Boat Deepener
(Deepener 1)
By Kyra Schaefer, CHI

As you continue to relax… breathing in and out in that way that feels comfortable to you…

Allowing your body to relax… even deeper… you rest in a beautiful cottage… that overlooks a large lake…

As you rest… looking out onto the vast lake, you begin to notice… there are a variety of sailboats… drifting… across… the lake…

You begin to notice… that on each sail… of each sailboat… is a number…as you look out, you notice a sail that has the number 10… written on it…

You feel your body relax even deeper…even more calmly… that boat floats away… and the next boat comes out with a number 9… on the sail. You notice that relaxation doubling…peacefully and easily…that sailboat drifts away…

The number 8 sailboat comes up… as you go deeper…and deeper down into relaxation… more peacefully and calmly…than ever before…

The number 7 sailboat drifts past… and you drift too… Relaxing every part of your body… d-e-e-p-e-r and d-e-e-p-e-r…

6… calm… effortless… relaxation… 5… d-e-e-p-e-r and d-e-e-p-e-r down…

4… c-a-l-m-e-r and c-a-l-m-e-r…

3… effortless… letting go… giving yourself permission… that this is what you want to do… to relax this deeply…

2… peaceful… calming… relaxation… fills every cell of your body…

And 1… all of the muscles in your body relax… every thought drifts… as you become… so calm…

Steps to the Beach (Deepener 2)
By Kyra Schaefer, CHI

Using your imagination... imagining that you are standing on a hill...overlooking the ocean...

The temperature is just right... the sun hangs low on the horizon... the sun's light is reflected like billions of diamonds... off of the ocean's surface...

You breathe in clean... clear... crisp... air. It feels good to you... to walk down to the ocean's edge...and you notice stairs leading down to the beach below.

You know that each step you take... is safe and calming... there are 20 steps that lead down to the beach below... you grab onto the handrail, and you step onto that 20th step... as you relax... deeper... and deeper...

19... you allow yourself to relax even more...

18... calmer and calmer...

17... each breath you take and each step you take... you find yourself doubling in relaxation...

16...

15...

14... every breath takes you d-e-e-p-e-r and d-e-e-p-e-r into relaxation...calm... effortless ease...

13...

12...

11... d-e-e-p-e-r and d-e-e-p-e-r down...

10... halfway to the beach now... so calm and relaxed...

9... give yourself permission... that this is what you want to do...8...

7...

6... you may notice your breathing has become even more peaceful andeasy...

5...

4...

3... calm... calm... relaxation...2...

And 1... drifting deeper and deeper... calmer and calmer... this is yourtime... this is your space for peaceful relaxation...

Cloud Count (Deepener 3) By Kyra Schaefer, CHI

Using your imagination... imagining yourself standing in a field.. all around you are tall grasses... trees... flowers... you are perfectly safe... there areeven open and clear spaces...

You bring with you... your favorite blanket and your favorite pillow... you unfold your blanket in the most perfect spot... just for you... to lay down...and relax...

The air is clean and crisp and clear... and it feels so nice... just take these few moments of peaceful relaxation...

As you lay down... you look up at the sky...the sky has multiple big fluffy clouds... these clouds seem to form the shape of animals... or trees... or other objects...

As you breathe in and out in that way... you begin to notice that the clouds begin to form into numbers...

The first cloud that floats by... forms into the number 18...

As a soft breeze blows... that cloud then turns into the number 17... and as it does... you find yourself becoming drowsy... comfortably drowsy... as you relax, those numbers... those clouds... help you to feel even more peaceful...

The breeze blows again, and the number 16 appears... as you relax... d-e-e-p-e-r and d-e-e-per... c-a-l-m-e-r and c-a-l-m-e-r...

15... deep... deep relaxation...

14... giving yourself permission... to go deeper into relaxation... 13...

12... calm.. peaceful... ease 11...

10...

9... d-e-e-p-e-r and d-e-e-per down... 8...

7... give yourself permission... to let go... you are always safe... peaceful and calm...

6...

5... deep... deep relaxation 4... calmer and c-a-l-m-e-r 3...

2...

And 1... that relaxation... moves throughout your entire body... as you drift deep... deep into relaxation now...

Forest Steps (Deepener 4)
By Kyra Schaefer, CHI

Using your imagination... putting yourself in a beautiful forest... the air is clean and clear... the temperature is just right... just the way you like it...

You look at all of the trees... their big broad leaves... you notice the sun shining through the leaves making little sun spots on the forest floor... it's the perfect day...

As you walk... you notice a large tree... probably the biggest tree you've ever seen... this tree is soo beautiful... you can almost feel... its energy of peace and relaxation...

As you walk towards this tree... you can sense your body relaxes more and more... you notice that as you walk to the tree... a door, at the base of the tree that's large enough for you to walk through... comfortably... safely... calmly...

As you walk through the door... you notice there are 20 steps that lead down... through the roots of the tree... and you can feel that there is something special at the bottom of these steps as you relax...

more and more effortlessly…

You step onto the 20th step, and you feel your body… immediately…relaxing…

You step down to the 19th step… d-e-e-p-e-r and d-e-e-p-e-r relaxation…18…

17…

16… c-a-l-m… peaceful.. e-a-s-e…

15… deeper and deeper down… into calming relaxation…14…

13…

12… peaceful… relaxing… effortless… calm… 11…

10… halfway down to the bottom now… giving yourself permission to let gocompletely…

9…

8…

7… calm… effortless…e-a-s-e…6…

5…

4… c-a-l-m-e-r and c-a-l-m-e-r…3…

2… letting go now… completely…

And 1… deep…deep… peaceful… relaxation…

Blowing Leaves (Deepener 5) By Kyra Schaefer, CHI

Using your imagination… allowing yourself to be outside on the most perfect Fall day… the temperature is just right… it feels so comfortable … so comfortable… and calming…

You notice a tree… and on this tree are many leaves that are ready to let go of their branches… and as you watch… you begin to notice… different leaves are beginning to fall… gently to the ground…

You catch your eye on a particular leaf… this leaf is attached to the tree…and you can get a sense of its desire to let go… to let go completely… as you too… wish to let go completely… with calm… effortless… ease… to feel that letting go and movement into d-e-e-p-e-r and d-e-e-p-e-r relaxation…

The wind blows gently, and you watch… how this leaf gently lets go… of its branch… it flows a little bit higher on the wind, and then you watch it drift…left to right… right to left… as it flows…

You become more relaxed… left to right… right to

left... following this leaf's peaceful journey toward the ground... left to right... right to left... so calm...so peaceful...

Giving yourself permission to let go now... completely... and easily... left to right.. right to left... deeper and deeper into relaxation now... and you know that when the leaf finally touches the ground, you will go... to that deep... deep state of relaxation... left to right... right to left... calmer and calmer... as the leaf gently touches the ground, you relax completely now...

Stepping Stone Bridge (Non-Process Deepener) By Carolyn Mackey CHT

Take a moment now to imagine you are on the shore of a glistening blue pond.

The pond is calm and inviting.

The temperature of the air is perfect. Just the way you like it.

You feel curious about this pond.

You begin by walking towards this beautiful, glistening pond. You walk all the way up to the edge of the gentle shore.

As you enjoy the peacefulness and the serenity of being by this pond, you notice a stepping stone emerge within a step from the shoreline.

This magical stepping stone is big, flat, and perfect for standing on. It emerges solid and sturdy. And it too is inviting.

You take a step with your right foot; then your left foot comes together.

As you stand on this stepping stone, on this

beautiful pond, you notice your feet become very, very relaxed. There is no tension in your feet anymore.

Then, another stepping stone emerges. You are interested in taking another step.

The pond is calm and glistening. It's so beautiful. And there is no one else around; you have this pond all to yourself.

You take another step. That's right.

With this step, you notice again; you feel very peaceful and calm. Upon taking this step, your knees soften and relax. You feel so good and so relaxed. More and more, with each passing moment.

The relaxation begins to travel up your legs.

You enjoy this relaxing sensation. The pond sparkles and glistens.

It's so peaceful and calm. Doesn't it feel good to relax?

Take some deep breaths, and enjoy this feeling…

Enjoy the sight of the pond—the sounds. And the smells of this magical, peaceful pond.

You look down, and you wait. You wait to see if there are any more of these magical stepping stones.

Yes, a new stepping stone emerges. Again, you take another step.

Wow, this stepping stone creates a very relaxed sensation in your thighs.

Your thighs and hips become very, very relaxed. This relaxation feels wonderful.

You feel confident and calm, and relaxed.

People do learn to help themselves relax using a relaxing visualization.

Another stepping stone has appeared. You are looking forward to continuing.

You continue to relax more and more, deeper and deeper.

You take another step.

You pause, smile, and wait for the relaxation to travel up your body, more and more.

Your belly button softens, the whole belly and back become very relaxed. The tension melts away.

It feels as if this sensation will last forever.

You allow this relaxing sensation to continue. It continues to make your entire body feel very peaceful and relaxed.

You could move if you needed to, but for now, you choose to just relax.

More and more.

Deeper and deeper.

More peaceful and more relaxed with each step.

Another stepping stone emerges. You're ready to take another wonderful step.

With both feet upon this next stepping stone, you feel your arms relax. They feel weightless.

Your body is now almost completely relaxed.

The temperature of the air feels perfect. This pond is calm and glistening.

It feels good to relax.

As you look down again for another stepping stone, you notice a shoreline. The shoreline is very close, but it is still a bit out of stepping distance.

You relax your gaze and breathe.

You feel so much relaxation throughout your body. One final stepping stone emerges.

You have one more chance to take another step. Another step of full and complete relaxation.

You take your last magical step.

You pause.

A wonderful wave of relaxation pours over the crown of your head. It covers your head and body with a warm, smooth sensation.

You are so completely relaxed.

This sensation can be felt throughout your entire body.

You're ready. You are ready to step back onto the land, relaxed, and ready to listen for the next instructions...

(Start script)

Abundance
By Jane Nelson, CHT

Now that you are completely relaxed, I want you to imagine abundance... (Pause) That's right ... anything that you can imagine... You are in a place of abundance... This is your sanctuary of abundance... a beautiful field... a field with shiny yellow grass as fine as silk. It is as soft as cashmere and feels as liquid as water. Each blade boasts its golden glow spun from the heavens...

This is your field of infinite possibilities... That's right... you can come here at any time and take all of the abundance that you need. It is given freely and without agenda. You can hear a gentle breeze sing its song of abundance.. and feel your hair being softly tussled around your face.

You feel lighter and happier than you have ever felt before...You feel relief...You breathe a long, slow, deep sigh of relief. Your entire being is filled with joyous laughter. You now acknowledge that debt is no longer a chain of darkness but freedom in the wisdom of all the ways that abundance is drawn to you and given to you...You feel a flutter of excitement about your future starting from right now standing in this field. This very second you feel safe. You feel confident with abundant confidence and happiness. You realize that you are loved and cared for and that you have all that you need.

Abundance is your divine right. It is yours in every way... embrace it... feel it...imagine it... the heaviness of blame is null and void. It no longer exists. You smile big and bright, realizing that abundance has found you. The wisdom is in your newfound confidence that you no live a life that is filled with all that you desire, and more you feel the soft golden grass sway against your bare legs. You touch the gentle grass with the palm of your hand, and it tickles. It feels so soft, clean, pure, silky it's so relaxing and soothing to the touch. It mesmerizes you. You slowly and gently pluck a long blade of grass. As you lift the golden thread of glass, a scroll silently flows out of the bottom, and the golden blade disintegrates into dust and effortlessly floats away in the breeze. With great anticipation, you slowly unroll the fragile scroll. The calligraphy is stunningly perfect, each golden letter, so perfect, you read, "Abundance has ALWAYS been yours." All you needed was a reminder of how to receive it. With great joy, your eyes begin to tear. You now understand it's absolute. Abundance is all yours, health all yours, love it's all yours, security, wealth and all abundance it's yours for the taking it's yours to share…. Whatever you desire in this field you can freely take with you... Now feel it… breathe in the abundance that is yours, fill your lungs with abundance, take one more slow, long, deep breath of all the abundance that belongs to you. Abundance is in all that you do… abundance IS… You lift your hands to the sky and wave gracefully and graciously. That's right, you raise your head and your face to the clear blue heavens… your eyes gently close, and you feel the warmth of the sun kiss your cheeks as you whisper…thank you. Thank you for abundance.

Abundance II
By Steve Haight, CHT

In a moment...we are going to plant a certain kind of seed, a seed of greatness, a seed that will change your whole world forever! But before we plant this seed, we must tend to the soil to make sure that the seed willgrow tall and very strong.

This seed has tried to grow in the past, but too many old things from the past poisoned and hardened the soil to the point that the seed could not grow. Take some time to Forgive the ground for being hostile to new growth and just remove and discard the old stones and contaminations. Washing away all the impurities, leaving only the freshest fertile organic soil.

This is the precious seed that has been guarded by the wealthiest of menthroughout the ages! Prepare yourself to receive it. The seed is this:

You must spend less money than you make. That's right simple and very powerful...less is more now. Just allow yourself to take in this precious seed to your most fertile soil, as you imagine tending to its every need. Using pure fresh water to encourage the seedling. You protect the seedling from all negativity because as you protect the seedling, it protects you! Watch how quickly and powerfully it grows! Growing...growing…growing tall and strong, into a mighty, mighty tree.

Now it provides shade and protection, and comfort. It provides all the fruit you need to thrive!! You and all your family! Watch as the tree grows so much larger. As it shares its fruit and produces new trees from its fruit... yes, even more abundance!!

Watch as those trees quickly grow, and they also cause even more trees to grow so tall and strong and abundant.

Faster and faster, the process grows. A forest of mighty trees. More andmore abundance now!

Imagine yourself enjoying all of the fruits of your labors. Now the trees take care of themselves.

You do so very, very well now!

The Achiever
By Bethany Orrick, CHT

Imagine yourself achieving at a very high level.

You are an achiever, motivated by success. You are well regarded, successful, productive, and efficient.

Your desire to achieve fuels your body and feeds you boundless energy. Your thoughts create an energy field around you designed for success.

From this moment forward, you are a very efficient, high-achieving individual. Your outlook for the future is very bright, and you can see only the success that is in your path.

Your motivation self-propels you to your future greatness.

Your thoughtful, practical mind will constantly be watching, helping you, and guiding you. You are a person who takes on responsibility and wears it well. You feel empowered by your achievements, and this propels you to do more.

You are extremely competent and have all the skills and ability to reach whatever goals you set.

You are a winner in life and are the creator of your universe.

Bedwetting Script
By Kyra Schaefer, CHI

Take a couple more deep breaths. That's good. You are getting more confident in staying dry more of the time. You know how good it feels when you wake up and the whole bed is dry. The sheets are dry and comfortable… And you snuggle into your soft pillow a little more, feeling good. In the past, you have woken up and felt really uncomfortable, now you wake up feeling confident and good. You are doing a good job of waking up in the middle of the night if you need to… to use the bathroom in the middle of the night if you feel the urge. You no longer drink water or anything before bedtime. You remind yourself of this every night… you use the bathroom every time you need to. You no longer hold your pee during the day… you use the restroom whenever you need to go. It's easy to wake up when you feel the urge to pee at night… at night, everyone is sleeping peacefully and continue to do so even if you flush the toilet… you use the bathroom in the middle of the night. You find your way easily, even if it's dark. When you go back to bed after successfully peeing in the toilet, you sleep very, very soundly and feel good when you wake up in the morning knowing you did such a good job. Imagine this you are accepting the award for being the best kid ever. You have a huge trophy that is golden and bright. You see all you're your family members and friends and classmates clapping and cheering just for you. You feel good and confident, in control. You did so good! You are staying dry every night. You picture yourself on your 7th (age-dependent) birthday, you are about to blow out 7 candles (or an appropriate number) on your delicious birthday cake, and before you blow them out, you realize that your wish came true. You are always dry. You can't remember a time that weren't dry. You always wake up feeling good and confident and strong. Like your favorite superhero (find out who that is), you are strong and tough, and nothing can keep you from having a dry bed when you wake up. It just always happens, a dry bed every morning. Even when you aren't home, even staying at a friend's house.

Your bed is always dry. You deserve that trophy. Imagine you are going to put that trophy in your room. You will remember that dry pants trophy every night. You did a great job listening today. You are a very good kid.

As a reward for doing so good, when I count to 5 and click my fingers, you will wake up feeling really, really good and excited. You may want to smile and laugh because you are such a good kid. Your parents are so proud of you, and they know you are doing a great job. Begin waking them up...

(It's ok if kids wiggle at first, usually they calm down after a few minutes. If you don't make it a big deal, they won't make it a big deal. If this script feels too long, some points can be adjusted. Most kids like the birthday and trophy image. Between ages 3-5, I teach the parents about sleep hypnosis, and I talk to them about changing daily habits, such as more frequent bathroom breaks, even if it means leaving class. Sometimes kids will hold it all day, which is hard on the body and will make them release at night without knowing it. We also have bed wetting alarms now built into blankets. That may be useful for the parent as well.)

Career Change
By Laura Post, CHT

Take a couple more deep breaths…that's good. You have hidden talents and gifts deep within you. They are stored in a secure box where you have kept them safe. It feels so good to see your box of talents and gifts. I'd like you to nod your head when you can see your box. That's right…there it is…so safe. You are so relaxed…so safe. Now I'd like you to imagine for a moment that you are opening the box and allowing your talents to rise…like a beautiful glowing light. The radiant light moves throughout your body.

Your talents and gifts are shining in every cell, from the top of your head to the tip of your toes. You feel more confident and more relaxed with all of your talents shining brightly. It feels so great to have your talents and gifts visible. You are safe…You are confident. You can see them clearly and can find them easily when you need them.

In the past, you have felt uncomfortable starting a new job, now you wake up feeling confident and in control. You naturally apply your talents and gifts to your new career. You are creative…you are open to new ideas…you have clarity, and you make good judgments. Yes, that's right…you have clarity, and you make good judgments.

Your talents and gifts are no longer stored in a box. You can use them anytime. You are successful…you are a leader…you shine brightly in your new career. You are doing great…take a deep breath. That's good.

When I count to 5 and click my fingers, you will come all the way back to waking consciousness, feeling confident, secure and with great clarity on your new career.

1…2…3…4…5

You have a strong mind.

Clutter-Free Living
By Shelly Marsh, CHT

I want you to use your imagination to create a new way to live because it is possible, isn't it? To live in a clutter-free organized home.

Imagine you unlocked the front door to your home.... and stepped into a freshly scented organized home. Imagine seeing your furniture in place.... there are cleared walkways.... table tops without clutter.... washed dishes.... and orderly kitchen counters. The heaviness you felt from clutter is gone. The shelves..... desks.... drawers and closets are orderly. You feel amazing. Items you seek are easy to locate. You spend less money because you know what you own. You feel relaxed and happy walking through your home.

Cast out clutter and welcome order into your home because it is possible, isn't it? You can start this today, or you can begin tomorrow. Give yourself permission to throw away broken items. You feel lighter as you place them into the garbage. You feel satisfied giving away things you no longer need to someone who needs them. You say yes to things you care about and noto things that outlived a purpose.

You feel powerful, liberating your home and your life. You find favorite items, a photo or jewelry perhaps, that you thought was lost forever. You reclaim the inner sanctums where you sleep, work and create. People do, you know, feel emotionally healthier in an organized home.

Removed clutter releases your frustration over unfinished projects. Gone is your guilt over undelivered good intentions. Gone is the tension in your body. You breathe with ease. (pause) Serenity and peace expand within you.

Clutter Script / Disorganization By Amanda Martin, CHT

Today is a day of new beginnings. Yesterday your environment was full of clutter, but today, _____(name), you've so bravely decided that it's ok to let go. You are so strong and so wise in making this decision. You have held onto old stuff – unneeded stuff – stuff that has no purpose and that has kept you in the past…but that was yesterday.

Right now, this very minute as you are hearing these words, your subconscious mind is hard at work. It is so powerful and so eager to please you that it is devising a beautifully and intelligently crafted plan. No longer is the needless accumulation of stuff necessary. No longer is it desirable.

Tell your subconscious… tell it silently… over and over, that you are now free. You are free from the burden of physical stuff. Thank you, mind and rest assured that your subconscious has already begun these changes. It has sent a message through every single fiber of your body. Every tissue and every single cell in your entire body has begun working together in complete harmony.

Physical clutter is mental clutter, and we know (name) that our mind is far too precious to poison with clutter. You have made this a priority, a commitment, and I want you to visualize your victory. Imagine now… imaging your home… completely free of clutter. What does it look like? I want you to imagine that you are standing outside of your front door. As you extend your arm to twist the handle to open the door, your eyes are immediately delighted. In that first instance, your first glance, you cannot contain your joy and excitement. This is your home. Take in its beauty.

Everything has a place, and nothing extra remains. Walk from room to room. Enjoy every single second. That's right. Take your time. This is your moment, and you've earned it. Thank your mind as you take 3 deep breaths. 1… you did an excellent job. 2… a bit deeper, and 3… congratulations. You may now open your eyes whenever you feel ready.

Confidence Boost
By Kim Balzan, CHT

Right now, I would like you to take a few deep breaths.... Just relax... This is your time to relax. Every time you hear me say the word You, you will feel more empowered. You should be proud of yourself... You are taking time to feel good about yourself... improve yourself... You are special... you are starting to feel more confident.

You are even starting to walk straighter... taller... your posture has improved and it shows... people are noticing something is different about you... You look important, powerful...

Your life has great purpose... You get excited now to talk and meet with others... because you know you are confident... you are moving forward... now it's easy for you to imagine doing the things you love to do... So easy... You see yourself doing it all... You look others in the eyes now and smile... feel how good it feels to have so much confidence... it's exciting, and you are doing it!

Now wherever you go, you feel comfortable ... you fit in.. you can see yourself in any situation having great confidence... any situation... life is good to you... you are starting to really appreciate who you are... you see how important you are to yourself and others... you love to even daydream and imagine a beautiful picture of you in your mind... confidence means so much to you.

You now feel like you are living the life you are meant to live... That's right, it has all happened all at the right time, it is your special time... you're so proud, that person that people are taking notice of is really you. Feel through your whole body what confidence feels like... you love that feeling.. it is here forever, confidence will always be within you ... imagine you were just filled up with all new cells and every one of them has confidence, strength, courage... how exciting to know, they are all for you and only you.

Diabetes: Type 1 (Insulin Dependent)
By Laura Post, CHT

You are here to become healthier…and the way you are going to accomplish this…beginning right now…is just by relaxing. Take a deep breath…that's right, you are going to just sit back and relax all the muscles in your body… that's good.

You are healthy and confident. You are whole and complete. You were born with the tools and knowledge to repair and restore. You know exactly what your body needs, and you accept the responsibility. In the past, you have felt unsuccessful, now you wake up feeling confident and good…accepting yourself just the way you are…healthy and in control.

You understand that you are in control of your body and how it functions each and every day. You are free of judgment and fear. You are in the driver's seat…and YOU are in control. You are doing a good job of testing your blood glucose levels when you need to…and it feels great to see those perfect numbers. You no longer worry or guess what is going on in your body. You are in control.

You easily pick the right foods and drinks to nourish your body. The food you are eating is fuel for energy and your good health. The food smells good, and every bite you take…it tastes good. You know exactly how muchinsulin your body needs to open your cells and allow the food to give you energy. You are in control. Nothing will keep you from eating healthy foodto fuel your body.

You no longer worry about complications because you are in control…you are making all the correct decisions for your health. You have acceptance …you are prepared…and you control your body. You will wakeup with more clarity and confidence and see your life in a new bright and radiant light.

Imagine for a moment…something that is of great importance to you, otherthan your health, that you are really proud of. Just relax and think about it for a moment. I want you to nod your head to acknowledge when you know what it is. That's good. I'd like you to continue to relax and without opening your eyes tell me what it is. That's right, great...now think about how wonderful you feel every time you think about yourself. From now on, you will feel the same joy and accomplishment that you feel right now each time you take care of your health. It feels so good...so safe...take a deep breath...that's right... you feel joy...you are proud...youare healthy, energized and whole.

When I count to 5 and click my fingers, you will come all the way back to waking consciousness, feeling healthy, confident and in control.

1...2...3...4...5

Feeding Horses
(Process Vehicle)
By Carolyn Mackey CHT

I want you to imagine yourself in a beautiful horse barn.

This is the largest, fanciest barn you've ever seen. From inside the barn, you can see a very long ally with many stalls. Each horse stall is closed and locked, but there is a small door in the upper right corner of each stall. This small door opens to a feed bunk. This is where the horses eat their grass hay for dinner.

In a moment, you are going to take a pitchfork and wheelbarrow full of grass hay, and you will feed all of the horses. Imagine this wheelbarrow is magic, and you never have to refill it. It just keeps replenishing on its own. You never have to stop to refill this wheelbarrow. Isn't that wonderful?

There are a total of 30 horses and 30 stalls. In a moment, you will begin by imagining yourself walking to the first stall on your left. You will open the mini-door, and with the pitchfork, you scoop grass hay from the magical bottomless wheelbarrow. Next, you will push the wheelbarrow from stall to stall, opening the feed bunk door, pitching scoops of grass hay into the feed bunk, and closing the door.

The first 10 stalls have ponies, and they only require one scoop of grass hay. The next 10 stalls are typical-sized riding horses. They each get 2 scoops of grass hay. And the last 10 horses are large, draft horses. They eat 3 scoops of hay for dinner.

You will imagine yourself feeding all of the horses, one at a time, being sure you give them the proper number of scoops. Ponies get one scoop, the riding horses get two scoops, and the working draft horses get three big scoops. Once you are done with the feeding exercise, you will feel relaxed enough to listen to the rest of the instructions. You will still hear my voice, but I'd like you to focus on completing the task. Don't listen to me again until the horses are all fed. Remember to feed each horse their appropriate portions. Try not to let any of the hay fall to the floor. When you have completely finished this exercise, you can relax and listen to the next instructions.

Begin now by pushing the wheelbarrow to the 1st

stall. Open the smaller feed door, pitch in one scoop of grass. Now, shut the door and move on to the next stall, without listening to me again, until all the horses are fed. Now on your own, go to the next stall, and with each horse you feed, you feel more and more relaxed. You are no longer focusing on my instructions; you are focused on finishing the task. With each door that is opened and closed, you grow calmer and calmer, and with each scoop of hay that is pitched you relax deeper and deeper.

The horses are so happy to be eating. This makes you feel good.

(Start Script)

Fear of Dogs
By Todd Schaefer, CHT

In the past, you used to feel afraid and anxious when you encountered a dog. You had that one experience that time of getting bitten (chased, barked at) by a dog, and so you felt hurt and afraid of all dogs after that. But now, you want to change that belief. You know that the world is full of dogs and that some dogs, somewhere, are nice, aren't they? Some dogs are very friendly and simply want to love you and show you their gratitude by licking you and wagging their tail to show you that they're happy. Some dogs are beautiful, and some smell really good, like they've just received a bath from their caring owner. You are taking an afternoon walk in the sunny park. You see an owner and his dog. This dog looks particularly pretty and has a coat that looks soft to the touch. This dog looks friendly and wants to interact with you. You ask the dog's owner if he is friendly, and the owner says that he is friendly. You ask if you can pet the dog, and with the owner's permission, you slowly approach the dog. The soft, furry dog gets excited because he knows that you are going to pet him, and he would love to interact with you. You gently pet his back and neck, and the dog enjoys it. You begin to feel happier from petting this dog, knowing that he loves you and knowing that you are safe petting this dog. You also begin to realize that people can be safe when they pet dogs. It's easy and fun to pet a friendly dog, isn't it? You start to feel so much better while petting this dog. This feeling better; it feels like confidence, doesn't it? You feel good about this dog, and you feel even better in realizing that future interactions with dogs can be safe for you, and you can feel enjoyment and increased confidence in every interaction. You say goodbye to the dog and its owner and continue your walk in the park, feeling elated about your positive experience and feeling that you can take that confidence with you into even more areas of your life because one confident experience makes you feel more confident in your next experience, whatever that may be.

You feel good now, and you enjoy dogs and lovely afternoon walks in the park. You enjoy the rest of your day feeling relaxed.

Finding Purpose
By Bethany Orrick, CHT

You are a beautiful, self-confident person with many skills and attributes. You have a purpose, and your purpose will make your world a better place. It is time to start searching for your true self. The self you desire to be.

The time is now to seek your purpose. Nobody is stopping you. You are confident and highly motivated. The world needs you to seek your purpose. As you seek your purpose, others around you will begin to start their journey towards their purpose. You will start a movement in your life. By seeking your purpose, you will motivate those around you to seek their purpose.

The energy you are creating is contagious, and you will change the energy of the atmosphere to one of success. You are very successful; no one can stop you from seeking your purpose. The change is happening in you now as I speak to you. From this moment forward, you are a confident person on the path to your purpose. You will overcome every fear and become stronger and stronger every day.

You are a confident, successful person on the path to your purpose. From this day forward, nothing and no one will get in your way. You will have the strength and courage to remove any obstacle that gets between you and your purpose.

Imagine your life with this new confidence. See how it feels. How light and airy you feel. Allow this new confidence to flow through your veins. Let this confidence lift you up when you have doubt and show you the way. From this moment forward, there is no barrier that cannot be overcome.

First Induction, Deepener & Awakening
By W. Randall Dunning, CHT

Let's begin your first hypnosis session by checking with your body to make sure it is in the best position to RELAX...check to make sure your arms and legs are uncrossed and your back, head and neck are comfortable...make any necessary adjustments now. It is unlikely that you will feel discomfort in your body as we go through our session, but if you do, you can gently and easily adjust for further comfort.

Now let's invite your body to relax. Go ahead; mentally say to your body... it's ok to relax. Allow your eyes to gently close... You are safe and comfortable. This is your time. Time for you. You deserve this time to let go of everyday concerns and just RELAX. Relaxation is easy. You don't have to do anything. Just allow it to happen. You can wonder how good it will feel in a few moments when you are completely relaxed. Each time you enter a hypnotic state, you will relax quicker and more deeply than the time before.

Focus on your breathing, in through your nose and out through your mouth. Notice how as you breathe in, your stomach rises, and as you breathe out, it contracts. Allow your breathing to go deeper....that's it. As I guide you, you will take 3 slow, deep breaths. Go ahead, take the first breath in slowly and out slowly...now take your second breath deeper...in...out...good. Take your third breath as deep as you can and then hold it for 3 seconds...one thousand, two thousand, three thousand...let it out slowly and completely...good....RELAX...deeper and deeper. Now breathe easily and comfortably. Notice how your breath is more shallow and effortless. As you relax deeper and deeper, I wonder if your body will feel heavy, or maybe you'll experience a floating sensation, or perhaps both.

Now let's talk to your body again, part by part. As we scan each part, mentally say to that part, "It's OK to Let Go." Invite your forehead and scalp to relax, releasing any remaining tension that may be there. Move your focus to your eyes and allow them to release. Relax your jaw, letting it hang open comfortably. You begin to notice a kind of flow to your relaxation. As your jaw relaxes, the relaxation starts to flow to your neck and then shoulders, which completely let go. Relaxation is flowing now to your arms, beginning with the top of your arms continuing down to your forearms... your hands... and your fingertips. Invite your chest to Let Go... your stomach muscles... your upper back... your lower back. The upper part of your body is now completely relaxed, but the flow continues to your pelvis and buttocks. As they release, you realize that your hamstrings and thighs are starting to relax, to let go. Feel the relaxation wave slowly making its way down your legs. Mentally thank your body for working with you to RELAX.

[*DEPTH TEST*] DEEPENER

Give yourself permission to use your imagination and inner vision. One of your trusted friends told you about a wonderful place that you could visit, and you have made the decision to check it out. Using your imagination, visualize a beautiful sunny day. The temperature is exactly like you prefer. There are scattered puffy white clouds in the blue sky. In front of you is an opening between some beautiful thick green bushes. As you walk toward the opening, you see a set of concrete steps going steeply down a hill. They are so steep you can't see all of them or the amazing place at the bottom, but you are very excited to explore them. In a moment, when you allow me, I will help you to climb down the steps. There are 10 of them in all. There's a metal hand railing you'll want to hold onto in order to steady your descent. Go ahead, grab hold of the railing.

As you take your first step...1...you may notice that your relaxation level is deepening. As you take your next step...2... You'll notice your body is continuing to relax deeper and deeper...3...going down...4...taking that next step...5...halfway down now...deeper and deeper...6...so relaxed...your feet are heavy on the steps...7... I wonder just how relaxed you will be when you get to the bottom. Almost there now...8...soooo relaxed...9...just one more step...10... You are now very deeply relaxed. In fact, you can't remember ever being so relaxed before.

[SUGGESTIONS SCRIPT]

AWAKENING

Now you realize your time here has come to an end. As you prepare to leave, the thought crosses your mind that every day, In every way, I am getting better and better. And as you ponder this, a large wooden exit sign crosses your line of vision. Underneath the word EXIT, a thick wooden arrow points toward an opening in the bushes. As you approach this opening, you notice that it looks very similar to the one you used to come down here…except that each step is twice as tall as the ones coming down. In fact, there are only 5 steps to get back to the top. You grab the handrail firmly with your left hand, and strrreeetch out your right leg to step up to the first step …1… you begin to feel the blood start moving in your arms and legs…step up ….2… starting to come out of hypnosis …3… your mind is alert …4… Your eyes are starting to open… 5…. Your eyes are wide open, fully alert. Wide awake, feeling rested and energized.

First Time Hypnosis Suggestion Script
By W. Randall Dunning, CHT

As you relax further, you realize that today's session is all about becoming familiar with hypnosis. You may not…or maybe you DO realize that hypnosis is a powerful tool to help you in directing your subconscious mind to make beneficial improvements to your life. Just to be clear…today…we are talking directly to your subconscious mind…NOW…

There are situations where being in a state of hypnosis is NOT helpful and can be dangerous, for instance, when driving a car or operating machinery. From today forward, you will be unable to enter a state of hypnosis when driving a car or operating machinery. Even if you're just feeling a bit drowsy while driving, your subconscious mind will prompt you to remain awake and aware until you can stop and rest or let someone else drive. In fact, your subconscious mind will alert you immediately when you are in a potentially physically dangerous situation, helping you to remain clear, calm and alert.

Right now, you are in a beautiful, safe and comfortable place. Do you remember? Look around and explore the special place you came to discover. When you made that last step down the stairs, you looked up and were amazed at the tranquil beauty you saw. This is your special place. Do you want to name it? You can call whatever you'd like...perhaps...Magic Lake...is a good choice. The grass is so lush and thick...flowers and bushes of every color and pattern...you are surprised by the pleasant aromas that fill the air. One aroma, in particular, draws your attention...it's your favorite flower scent...you walk over to it...bend down and breathe it in DEEPLY. It always brings you the feeling of PEACE and CALM...relaxing you deeper and deeper.

As you stand up and turn, your attention is drawn to the crystal clear lake. The water is so calm it looks like a mirror...a mirror reflection of the puffy whiteclouds, the sun and even the blue color of the sky. You're curious...what is the temperature of the water? You walk over to the water's edge ...bend overand touch it... perfect... it's the perfect temperature. You make a mental note to bring a towel next time you visit to dry off after your swim. Have you become aware of the sounds yet?... The water is lapping gently on the shoreline, the birds singing, the soft breeze rustling the leaves...the music of nature. You just want to lie down, RELAX, and take it all in...so you do. The thick grass is almost like a featherbed. You decide to lie there for a few minutes and enjoy. Go ahead; take in the sights...sounds...smells...as you become even more relaxed. (Let them rest without talking for 1 to 2 minutes.)

AWAKENER

Gratefulness Script
By Tibbeth Jordan, CHT

As your continue to drift down into this soft state of relaxation, you are aware of your breathing. Feel yourself inhale the strong sense of gratitude, and when you exhale, do so slowly: relaxing in this strong sense of peace. As I speak these words, quietly repeat them in your own mind and embrace their meaning fully. I am grateful for these hands that serve me every day. I am grateful for my eyes that allow me to see the beauty in the world. I am grateful for my arms that allow me to hold those so dear to me. I am grateful for my legs that carry me throughout my day with such ease. I am grateful for my lungs that so easily pull in the oxygen needed to support my body. I am grateful for the dedication of my heart that beats for me so consistently and allows me to give and receives such a strong sense of love. From this moment on, I choose to live my life with gratitude and see beauty in the many joys of life.

Healing and Peace During Pregnancy
By Kate Nethercott Wilson, CHT

Now remaining completely calm and relaxed, I want you to imagine or sense that you are surrounded by a beautiful ball of healing and protective light. And as you take a deep breath, imagine or sense the color of the light, knowing that whatever color you choose is perfect for you and your baby. And now, imagine this light surrounding your body, and as you breathe in, it fills each and every cell of your body with a feeling of calm and peace. You and your baby are completely protected and safe surrounded by this light.

Now in just a moment, I'm going to invite you to use the light to release and let go of any fears and worries that you may have about pregnancy and childbirth, beginning with your own birth. Remaining completely calm and protected by the light, allow yourself to see, feel or just get a sense of your own birth. Good, that's right. Now allow the healing, peaceful light to dissolve any and all fears, disappointments or un-supportive beliefs that you or your mother may still carry from your birth. As you do this exercise, you may not understand how the light is healing your birth experience but just know that at a deep level, it is.

Good, now taking a deep breath, I want you to imagine or sense your grandmothers and any other of your female ancestors joining you and your mother in this beautiful healing circle of light. Taking a few moments to allow the light to release and let go of any negative birth experiences that these women may have had...... Now releasing family patterns, family fears, beliefs or worries about pregnancy and childbirth that you and the women in your family no longer need to hold on to. You will know exactly what needs to be released, and you will let go with ease. You have many strong female role models in your family past and present. You know that at any time during your pregnancy, you are able to draw upon their strength and experience by simply closing your eyes, going within and connecting to the mother wisdom that is already inside you.

Good.....now it's time to release and let go of any and all worries you may have related to what other people have told you about pregnancy and childbirth. You may have friends or colleagues who have had negative pregnancy or birth experiences. If anyone comes to mind, just bring them into the light. Good…..You know that other people's experiences and fears have absolutely no influence upon you, your pregnancy or the birth of your child. You listen to your intuition and acknowledge all your feelings; however, your inner confidence is unwavering. You are truly empowered to make all of the right choices for you and your baby, easily and comfortably. You know with confidence that pregnancy and **childbirth is a natural, normal event in your life.** You trust that you already know what is best for you and your baby. Your baby is like no other, and you are meant to be together.

Good, now as you keep focusing on breathing in the light surrounding your body, you will continue to release and let go of any and all beliefs and patterns about pregnancy and birth that are not supporting you. You know that your baby picked you and that you are the perfect mother for this baby. This is the perfect time for you to be pregnant. Your baby is growing inside you stronger and stronger every day. As you move through your pregnancy, it is easy for you to nurture your body with healthy foods and exercise.

You honor your body and the changes it is going through to bring your baby into the world. You make time to move your body each day, and you love your body, knowing that it is supporting and protecting your baby. Isn't it amazing the way your body adapts perfectly in support of you and your baby? You know that you are truly blessed to have this baby.

During your pregnancy, you allow yourself time each day to focus on renewing and nurturing yourself. Even though you may be busy balancing many things in your life, you trust that all the necessary purchases and preparations will happen at the right time, and you can remain relaxed and enjoy this beautiful time of preparation for you and your baby. With each day of your pregnancy, you feel better and better, and you experience more peace and joy, knowing your baby is closer and closer to being born.

Still breathing in the light, you completely let go of any desire to control the process of your pregnancy and birth. You know that your pregnancy and the birth of your baby will be perfect for you both. During your pregnancy and as your baby is born, you are able to remain relaxed and calm because you trust that you and your baby know exactly what to do.

Now you are completely calm and at peace with your pregnancy. You are exactly where you are supposed to be. This is the perfect time for you to bepregnant and the perfect baby for you. You have all of the tools, wisdom and knowledge within you to provide for this baby. You chose to surround yourself with nurturing, supportive people around at this important time in your life.

As you move forward in your pregnancy, you will continue to feel this peace...you will feel this peace during childbirth, and you will feel this peacewhen your baby is with you. Your thoughts and feelings about your pregnancy and childbirth are completely positive and peaceful.

Healing Athletic Injuries
By Freddy Sandoval, CHT

I am healthy because every day, I take care of my body by committing 100% to doing my exercises in the training room. I understand that my body reacts to my thoughts; therefore, I choose to think only positive thoughts. I concentrate solely on the task I am doing, focusing all my attention on my breathing and allowing my body to heal on every breath. I inhale positive thoughts and exhale the natural body waste, therefore, allowing the blood to flow smoothly through my veins all the way back to my heart. I can feel the swelling go down while my blood flows smoothly from my injury to my heart. I am relaxed, positive, and I truly believe I am in control of my healing. In four weeks from today, I am back on the field, playing at my best because I am healthy and strong.

Today, I am healthy because I am in control, and I choose to heal my body. Today, I concentrate on doing each and every single one of my exercises in the training room because I know they are good for me and because they make me stronger. Today, I allow the blood to flow smoothly from my injury all the way back to my heart, releasing all the body waste from my injury and allowing my injury to heal. Today, I choose to be positive all day, constantly healing my body with the power of my mind in every breath that I take. Today, I am healthy because I am a big-league player.

Insecurity
By Rita Lake, CHT

As I speak to you, your body and mind will relax…Take a deep breath and slowly exhale.. take another deep breath and exhale… now you can let go deep into… a comfortable relaxation…. causing your body to feel free of all thoughts. Now bring your attention to your breathing… see your breath going into you and leave.

Relax, take a deep breath and relax deeper, now as you take a deep breath, see yourself relaxing deeper and deeper… now see yourself becoming more and more relaxed and feeling more comfortable.

Now repeat these words to yourself……I am wonderful……I am outstanding….

I am worthy……

I will be successful in everything I do…now imagine seeing yourself secure… successful. See yourself attracting successful people all aroundyou. You are secure…. You are successful… you are brilliant.

Now that you have an idea of what you want… see yourself being all these things.

Loving Yourself
By Andria M. Pacinelli, CHT

As you continue to relax deeper, I want you to focus on the words that I'm saying. That's right, just let yourself relax and focus only on my words…nothing more. Let go of any outside distractions. Let go of any other thoughts or feelings that may be clouding your mind. Don't worry about anything….just focus on my voice and the words that I'm saying.

From this day forward, you will see yourself as the wonderful and amazing person that you are. You will no longer harbor any bad or negative feelings about yourself because we know that those thoughts and emotions have no positive purpose here. You are no longer going to think of yourself as anything less than perfect just the way that you are, and you will not allow anyone else's actions to bring you down. You feel strong, beautiful and secure. You enter each day with confidence and love….love for yourself and love for all of those around you. You know that you are a wonderful, loving being, and you have so much respect for yourself. You care about your body, the temple that houses the essence of who you are, and you take wonderful care of your body. You are conscious and thoughtful about your body and what you put into it. You are thoughtful about the foods you eat because you know that eating healthy is good for your body to keep it strong and functioning well. Because you take such good care of your body and because you feel the warm and comforting love that you have for yourself easily and regularly, you are relaxed and happy. You experience joy and live a life based on a foundation of love. You know that you are worthy of receiving love just as you are able to give it. As easily as you are able to love outside of yourself, you are also loving yourself. You are loving your wonderful, kind, compassionate and confident self, and you respect every aspect of you.

Low Self-Esteem
By Mary Stoner, CHT

You are joyful, positive, energetic, and feeling free. All of your thoughts are positive because you know that today will be a fantastic day. Anytime someone says something negative to you, your subconscious mind will cancel the statement and not accept it…You deserve happiness…You are a unique amazing being…You have talents and gifts that no other person has. You see yourself as the loving, beautiful person that you know you are. When you walk out the door and go about your day, it's really no big deal because you are ready to face anything with perfect confidence. There is nothing anyone can say or do to bring you down. You feel enthusiasm and confidence in all that you do. Friends and family enjoy your company because you radiate your beautiful love and peace outward effortlessly.

You enjoy speaking to other people, and sharing experiences is no big deal because you know every word spoken is genuine. When people see you, they think, wow, what an amazing beautiful bright light. From this day forward, you will be self-confident… capable… determined. You love yourself...

You are an important and valuable person.

Nail Biting
By Jane Nelson, CHT

As you continue to drift down deeper into complete relaxation... Imagine your hands with strong, manicured, beautiful nails. You are thrilled and excited with new confidence and happiness about making this change. You have decided to let your nails grow and take good care of them. Your skin around your nails will be healed and smooth as silk. The negative behavior and embarrassment of nail-biting is a part of your past. It no longer exists.

You will find positive ways to deal with stress and moments when you feel anxious. When you feel like bringing your hands close to your face, you will instead place them on your heart... feeling yourself breathe sloowww calm... relaxed... feeling your heart's pace slow, reminding you that you are in complete control... you have the power to find positive solutions.... and you are making this change. You feel happy that you don't have to worry about germs being transmitted through nail-biting. You see the beautiful relaxing salons where you can be pampered when you don't feel like manicuring them yourself. You feel the slow…deep… incredibly relaxing hand massage… the warmth of the towels that penetrate deep into your bones… so relaxing…so comfortable, and your hands and nails are beautiful and so healthy. You have chosen to perceive things differently so that you are less stressed and more powerful… always in control… you have all the control…total control… so powerful to change this habit of nail-biting… it's gone… no longer exists…because you have made this change… you are in control… that's right, total control.

Owning Your Own Emotions – Too Emotionally Invested in a Relationship
By Amanda Martin, CHT

In a moment, I am going to ask you to do something that has always proved very difficult for you. Sometimes you have even felt it to even be impossible. However, that was your old way of thinking and your old way of feeling. In the past, you have allowed yourself to emotionally bond with someone so strongly, too strongly… and too soon, and it has really hurt you. It has caused you a great amount of pain and loss, and heartache. But today, you are going to take all of those feelings back. You are going to accept them, you are going to own them, and then you are going to LEAVE them. You are going to leave all of these negative feelings, and you are going to leave them forever. From this moment on, you will never, ever allow hurtful thoughts to enter into your head. No one can hurt you unless you allow them to. NO ONE can hurt you…unless…you allow them to. In life, we get what we tolerate, and today, you will tolerate it no more, and you will invite it in no more. Not even one single time.

In a moment, I am going to ask you to take three very deep breaths. Before I do that, I am going to assure you that you can do this. You CAN do this.

Your mind really CAN do absolutely anything that it desires to do, and this is an incredible power, a power that you yourself hold. This moment is not about anything else – it's simply about your ability to take control over your emotions and to own them. They are your own. No one…NO ONE can lead you to feel anything that you won't allow them to. Owning your emotions has been hard in the past, but not today and not right now. Right now, you are strong and confident and able. You CAN do this.

If you are ready, I would now like you to begin taking three deep breaths. With each exhale, I want you to push all of those hurtful feelings that have been building up out. 1… you feel so much better already. 2… you are allowing only positive feelings and thoughts. 3… push them out with all of your heart and with all of your mind. You don't need them. YOU are everything that you will ever need to be complete. As we conclude, I am going to count to five slowly. As I do, I want you to repeat what I am saying inside of your own head. Say these following five things directly to your subconscious and say them with authority. Own these five things, and your emotions will no longer own you.

1... I am strong-minded.

2... My mind and my mind alone controls my emotions.

3... MY mind is more powerful than any other force imaginable.

4... I choose to love my mind and thank my mind, and nourish my mind with only the best of thoughts.

And

5... When I do these things, my mind will give me a healthy release of emotions.

As we conclude, I would like to remind you that your subconscious is like a 4 yr old child. Children must be nourished and showered with positive praises and unconditional acceptance. But unlike a child, who is not perfect, your mind is perfect. It is absolutely perfect in every single way, which means that it will record every positive but also every negative thought, feeling and emotion. From today on, you will shower your mind with unconditional love so that it will perfectly record and accurately demonstrate how amazingly incredible YOU are.

Whenever you feel ready, you may begin to open your eyes.

Professional Baseball Confidence
By Freddy Sandoval, CHT

I am healthy because I take care of my body every day. I understand that my body reacts to my thoughts. Therefore I choose to think only positive thoughts. I am the most positive person in the world. I am always relaxed, positive, and confident in my ability to play baseball because I trust myself and I believe in myself. I am the best player in the organization because every day, I choose to work harder than anyone else on the field. I am strong, powerful, positive and confident. I take pride in what I do, and day in and day out, I lay it all on the field because I am the best. I am in control of my thoughts and my body, and I choose to give my absolute best in everything I do. I understand that no one is perfect; therefore, I choose to beexcellent and excel in everything that I commit to doing. I love baseball because I have fun, because I am great at it and because I enjoy it.

Every day I show up to the field ready to compete, ready to win the daily battle, to outwork everyone, and to be the best player I can be. I stick to my routine every day because it makes me comfortable because it makes me strong, because it makes me better. I am a warrior, a gladiator ready to fight.

Today, I am relaxed, positive, and confident in my ability to play baseball. Today, I am in control of everything I do, in control of my positive thoughts, in control of my actions and ready to succeed. Today, I choose to give my absolute best in everything that I do. Today, I allow myself to play at my maximum potential because I am comfortable, positive, confident and moreprepared than anyone else. Today, I am the best baseball player on the field because I choose to be.

Releasing a Romantic Relationship
By Kyra Schaefer, CHI

Take an additional deep breath. That's good. You are letting your body relax to the deepest level it feels comfortable with. I'll invite you to let these ideas wash over you like a warm bath. You are whole. You have everything you need with you. Nothing has been taken away because… you are letting go of this relationship. As you feel these ideas move to the deeper parts of your understanding, you may start to feel a bit of expectancy for the possibilities in your future. People come into our lives for a season, a reason, or a lifetime. If they come into our lives for a season, it means they were only meant to be here for a certain amount of time, and now it's time for them to move on. If they are here for a reason, it could be that you are learning to let go and move forward. And for those that are here for a lifetime, we reserve this special place for our closest friends and family members and sometimes romantic relationships. A season can last a long time or a short time. A reason could pass in a moment if you have learned a lesson, and a lifetime is that feeling like you know them because they area part of you. These are the people that can always be depended upon.

They tend to be those that created you and helped you learn and grow from an early age. You have a person in mind now that fits into one of those categories. As you feel it's right, let yourself know which one they are now. As you designate a category for them, I want you to imagine that you are sitting across from them comfortably in a chair. You can see them, and they can see you. Say what you need to say that will take you to the place of closure that you need to be. Thank them for being in your life, and tell them that now it's time to finish the relationship and let them go. Imagine any negative cords you have running between the two of you. Ask your powerful subconscious mind what tool it would like to use to cut and destroy these cords completely. (**sometimes people will say they don't want to cut the positive cords, I keep reminding them these are the negative cords only, I usually ask them to describe the cords color, texture and what they use to cut the cords**) Once all the cords are cut, take the ends of the cords and destroy them in whatever way your subconscious mind would like to do it. (**I ask the client what they use. Usually, it's by burning**

them up. I remind them that nothing is left of the cords, no ashes or even burn marks.) Thank the person for being there with you and tell them farewell.

Bring your attention back now to your breathing. Let's get back to your body and mind. Feel that good breath moving through your lungs and imagine that you are in the most beautiful place ever imagined, and it's 6 months from now. There is a sense of empowerment that moves through your whole body... from the top of your head down toward the bottoms of your feet. You are gaining confidence with each breath you inhale. You are now in this beautiful place, and you are looking back in your imagination to 6 months ago. You laugh to yourself a little bit because you realize you haven't thought of that person at all since you were in the office with the hypnotist. You realize that you have felt more confident every day, and every day your good feelings have increased. It's almost as if that person was simply eased from your mind. It feels so good to know you have let them go completely. What was their name? It seems the more you try to remember, the more it escapes you. It feels like a lifetime ago. You breathe deeply and remember you are powerful, you are in control, and you feel good more of the time since you let go and created this perfect and peaceful life. Your body is healthy, you are radiant, you shine with a brightness that everyone sees and can experience. See yourself new now. Feeling better and better.

When I count to 5 and click my fingers, you will come all the back to wakingconsciousness, feeling so good, so powerful, so delighted in your newfound awareness of yourself. You are clear and know what you need to do. Start counting… bringing them back.

School Performance
By Andria M. Pacinelli, CHT

You are calm, relaxed and in control. You are confident, and you are in control of all that you do. From this moment on, you are able to concentrate so much better than ever before. You believe in yourself, and you know that you have the skills that you need to succeed. You are equally as smart as all of your peers around you. You feel confident in yourself and your ability to do well in school. You know that anything you attempt to do, you will give it 100%, and you are sure that you will succeed. You feel confident at school, and your schoolmates look up to you. They see you as someone who is intelligent, kind and determined to succeed.

Your peers admire you for asking questions in class because that shows your courage and determination to learn. You concentrate easily, and you can effortlessly access all of the information you learn in school at any given time. You are able to concentrate and focus in school because you are giving it your full attention. By doing so, you find it more enjoyable.

You find your studies and projects interesting, and you are able to focus somuch more easily than ever before. Your new ability to concentrate and your confidence about being successful in school allows you to learn so easily, and you can remember what it is you are studying or learning effortlessly. With this amazing and wonderful ability to remember information about what you've learned so effortlessly, so easily, that you find test-taking to be a fun experience in which you excel. You take tests with ease. You are confident, calm, focused, and prepared. Because you concentrate so easily and have the amazing ability to access the memory of what you've learned, you experience the joy and satisfaction of getting good grades. Seeing your assignments come back to you with good grades makes you feel happy. You are so proud of the wonderful job you've done, and those around you are proud of you too.

Your mind is the most perfect computer in existence. Your computer is now able to concentrate and remember more easily and effortlessly thanever before…and this new gift will remain with you throughout your life because you are interested…because you see its value…it's wonderful to be able to take in information…to learn new things and to be able to remember that information so easily when you need it. You can feel confident about school and know that you will do well. Just because you may not know something doesn't sway you. You are open-minded, and you know that when you focus your attention, you can learn easily and succeed. You have a strong and amazing mind.

Self-Confidence
By Karen L Chaney, CHT

Imagine you are riding in a car with your friends. It's evening, and you are all going to a party. You are wearing your favorite outfit. You are all talking and laughing in the car, but somewhere inside, you are a little nervous about being out with strangers. As you ride along, your friends tell you this will be lots of fun, and they are excited about meeting new people. You become just a little excited too. Maybe this won't be so bad.

Now you are at the party and just about to go in. You hear the music and know there are a lot of people inside. You see them in your mind dancing and talking together, smiling and laughing. They are having a good time. Imagine that when you enter the room, some turn to look at you and your friends and others don't seem to notice. It's ok. When they look at you, some may have been waiting for you and your friends, and others may be looking to see if they know you. They notice what you are wearing, and it's ok if they like it or if they don't like it, you like it.

You are at the party, and your friends have gone off to talk to others. You are relaxed and feeling good. You look around and find someone to talk to. You don't know anyone, but that is ok. You are giving them the chance to get to know you too. You will find someone in the crowd that you feel safe talking with. You know best who is a safe person for you to be around.

Once you have found that person, you go to introduce yourself.

As you are talking to this person, a part of your mind notices that this isn't so bad. In fact, this feels really nice. You may not agree with everything the person is saying, but you like being confident and comfortable around them. You decide to move to another person, and the conversation becomes easier and easier with each new person you meet.

Now you are with your friends again, getting ready to leave. You leave the party and get into the car and start driving home. You are all laughing and talking about the party. You are comfortable and relaxed talking about all the new people you have met, sharing comfortably and easily with your friends.

Self Love, Self Worth
By Shelly Marsh, CHT

I want you to take a deep breath. You are going to give a wonderful gift to yourself. You will use your imagination to define and embrace your true self-love.... and self-worth.... because it is possible, isn't it.

Imagine it is daylight, and you are sitting on a comfortable log beside a stream in the woods. You see the water playfully tickle the rocks while trickling downstream. The sun's muted heat feels good on your shoulders as you sit under a canopy of a tree. At your feet is a box decorated in gold foil and flowers. You open the box. Inside is a soft, elegant...blue topaz-colored shawl created just for you. Three messages are woven into the shawl. As you read the words, they are stitched into your mind and your heart.

"Trust yourself and release worry around trusting others."

"Take care of yourself and release disappointment when others do not meet your expectations."

"Speak your truth, and do not worry what others

think."

You feel heady with knowledge. You give yourself permission to accept the gift. You wrap the shawl around you and receive a hug from the deepest source of love imaginable.

A breeze moves the trees reminding you that your past no longer serves a purpose. You release destructive thoughts and memories into the stream. They make a 'plunk' sound falling in the water. Thestream carries them away from you.

You feel lighter. The past has no power over you.

You will BE yourself,…SAY what you mean…. and DO what you love.

You will start this today or begin this tomorrow. You will sparkle even more brightly on this earth because this is possible, isn't it?

The words on the shawl are now wisdom you command. You love yourself deeply. You feel amazing. You ARE yourself,….you SAY what you mean…. and LOVE what you do.

You love yourself…..

without judgment ….

without penalties….

without limitationsor fine print.

You are perfect…and perfectly beautiful because it is possible, isn't it. Happiness shines within you and outward, much like a large star at midnight. You have claimed your self-love and defined your worth. Shine on.

Feelings of Unworthiness Script By Garvin De Shazier, CHT

Now, as you breathe evenly and easily, I invite you to take one extra deep, cleansing breath ... and as you exhale, let your breath flow smoothly and easily away from you... let it carry away any tension you may have... and now just breathe normally and easily.

As you look back on your life, [name], you begin to see that every time someone said something to you or behaved toward you in a way that felt hurtful to you; it was always about their emptiness ... You understand now that all of them were struggling just to cope with their own lives... and that they were simply lashing out at you as a convenient target... every time they hurt you, it was accidental, even when it seemed like they were doingit on purpose... The things they said or did that caused you to question your own worth were all just unintentional lies... told to you by people who simply did not know any better.

You can see it now, can't you, [name]?... They all thought they were right, but you can see it more clearly now, can't you, [name]?... People make mistakes, don't they?... And, sometimes those mistakes hurt other people, don't they?... But, that doesn't make them evil or worthless, does it, [name]?... In fact, you sometimes make mistakes, but now you know that mistakes are just a way to learn and grow, aren't they?... That's how babies learn to walk, isn't it, [name]? Babies don't just jump up and start running, do they?... They stand up and then fall down a few times, don't they?... But, then what do they do?... They pull themselves up and try again, don't they?... And they keep on getting back up, every time they fall, even when it hurts until they find their balance and learn how to walk, don't they?... You can see that cute little baby now, can't you?

That's how it is with all kinds of mistakes, [name] ... You have the ability to learn from your mistakes, and from the mistakes of others, even when those mistakes hurt you... In fact, this ability to learn from mistakes is one of your great strengths, isn't it?... When you make a mistake, you can accept that you are just learning a new lesson... and you are grateful for your ability to learn... because learning always makes you stronger, doesn't it, [name]?... And when someone else makes a mistake, you canbe compassionate to them, can't you?

And when you're compassionate to another person, that means you care about them, doesn't it?... Just like other people care about you, [name].

...You've touched so many people's lives, [name], many people you didn't even realize you were touching... So many people are grateful for you and the ways you've touched their lives ... Maybe they've never told you, but they do care about you ... You would be amazed if you knew how many people do care about you!

[name], I know that sometimes you may have had thoughts that you weren't good enough... But, you can see now that that's a lie, too, can't you?... You remember hearing about one of the wisest men who ever lived, Albert Einstein, don't you?... He said, "You can look at life as if nothing is a miracle, or as if everything is a miracle."... You can see now that everything is a miracle, can't you, [name]?... And, if everything is a miracle, that means you, too, doesn't it?... You can see that you are a special, unique and magnificent expression of God's creative love... You're the only person exactly like you that has ever existed, since the beginning of time, so God must have had a really good reason for creating you, didn't He? ... Your life is a precious gift, isn't it [name]? ... And, you get to choose how you will invest every single day

of the rest of your life.

Whatever you have believed about yourself in the past in now in the past, [name]... from this moment forward, you now see yourself as worthy of the best life you can possibly have... you see yourself as capable of making wise and empowering choices... you see yourself as kind and compassionate and understanding of yourself and others... you enjoy the feeling of doing kind things for others, and you recognize that your kindness is an expression of the worthy person you are, [name].

When you awaken from this trance, you will feel confident and self-assured

... you will be energized and alert, and you will remember that you are kind and compassionate to others... Now, I'm going to count to five, and you will awaken as soon as you hear the word "five." ... One, you are becoming aware of the room around you... two, you start to notice your breathing... three, you start to feel energy flowing throughout your face and hands and your whole body... four, your eyelids want to open now... and five, you are now fully conscious, and you feel wonderful!

Sewing Improvement
By Connie Brown, CHT

Just take a few more deep breaths. That is good. Now see yourself in a big sewing room. There are machines, beautiful bright colors of treads and material on a big table. You thirst for sewing information. You have a desire to be creative and be original. You want to sew just for the sheer fun of it.

You will surely gain a special reward of self-satisfaction. You walk over to the big table and pick out your favorite color of material to work with. Then you pick out a thread color to match perfectly to your material on the big table. Then put your pattern on top of the material, pinning them together, and cutting out each piece. You can see in your mind's eye your finished product. You are excited as you walk over to the sewing machine with your material and supplies in hand. You pull out your chair and sit down and take a deep relaxing breath. The feel of the material is perfect for this project. "You know that each project can have several thousand stitches, and with each stitch, you create you are becoming more confident in your abilities." You start the machine, sewing one side and then the other, and then put it all together. You see everything coming together. "See your finished project, run your hand across the beautiful work that you have created, feeel the texture. Take a deep breath, knowing you have created something that will keep someone warm and feeling loved." You put on the last finishing touches. It is wonderful. You are very satisfied with your work. You see yourself as someone that can sew.

Now take a deep breath and count from 4 to 1, and with each count, you will begin to come back to your waking state. Feeling delighted that you can now sew. And you are clear on what you need to do.

(Awakening)

Smoking Cessation
By Leslie Freidlander, CHT

You are here with me feeling deeply relaxed ... feeling positive because you are choosing to end your cigarette smoking habit. You can feel proud of yourself now that you are taking this step toward better health.

Your health is important to you. Imagine yourself having more energy to do all the things you want to do. Imagine being able to breathe deeply and fully, smelling the beautiful scent of the fresh air.

I completely understand how you may want that cigarette after dinner or with your coffee, but pleasant company and good conversation after dinner would be nicer, would it?

Remember back before you started smoking how wonderful food smelled and how tasty it was. It will be that way again when you leave smoking behind. I know this is something you want to release and let go. And that is what you are doing.

Each day you will feel less and less like smoking. Less and less time thinking about it. Less and less. Every day your home will smell cleaner and cleaner.

It's a weight off your shoulders. You feel confident that you can move forwardnow as a non-smoker.

Picture yourself spending the money you used to spend on cigarettes on something just for yourself as a reward. Each time you do, you will feel pride inyour success as a non-smoker.

Smoking Cessation II
By Shirley Dunlap, CHT

You're nice and relaxed. That's right, relaxed from the top of your head to the bottom of your toes. This is exactly where you want to be. It has taken great effort on your part to get this far in the process, and now you can feel extremely proud that you've decided to take the first step towards stopping smoking. You're still very relaxed, and that's good, stay relaxed so that we can concentrate on the important first step of stopping smoking.

From now on, you will visualize yourself as a non-smoker. You will not be able to imagine holding a lit cigarette in your hand between your fingers. Your hands will now always be free to use their dexterity in a number of other ways. It feels so good for your hands to always be free and to not hold a cigarette. Never again will you drop a cigarette and burn your clothes or your car seat, the carpet. You are a non-smoker.

Now you can go to the movies without standing outside just before the movie starts to have that last cigarette before going into the theatre. And once you're inside, nothing will be on your mind except the movie. You will never have a thought that the movies seem long, simply because you are getting anxious to be outside again. That's right, the movie is a comfortable place to be, and you feel so very relaxed and at ease while watching the movie. You have so much confidence in yourself now that you do not have a dependence on something that has basically ruled your life in the past.

If you find you need to travel by air, you are comfortable anticipating a five-hour flight knowing that you will feel relaxed and at ease the entire time, never feeling uncomfortable because of restrictions on board. You are free. You feel so good, so relaxed, so relieved of what used to rule your life. Now you make plans based entirely on what you want to do. You never plan something according to where you might be and how long you will be restricted or where you could smoke. You are a non-smoker. There is no reason for you to care. You feel so free, so relaxed, and so proud.

When you took that first step to stop smoking, you learned many things that will make the process easier. You know that nicotine only stays in your system for three days. After only three days, your system is free of nicotine, and you cannot imagine why you would ever feed your body nicotine again. It feels so good to have your body free of nicotine. You're feeling so good, so pure. You also know that an urge to smoke only lasts three minutes.

You know how strong you are, and you know how determined you are. You are of such a strong mind you know you can keep yourself busy and pass three minutes without any trouble. Then you find that as you make yourself busy for only three minutes each time you have that urge, you now find the urges becoming fewer and farther between. You used to think of it once a half hour. Now suddenly, an hour passes, and you didn't even realize that you hadn't even thought of smoking. You are a non-smoker, and it feels so good. So wonderful. Now the urges are two and three hours apart, and before you know it, you have had an entire day pass without even thinking of smoking. That's right because you are now a non-smoker. This is such a wonderful accomplishment.

Your clothes smell good. There is no residual smoke odor on your clothes, in your car or in your house. Everything smells so good and so fresh.

Suddenly you realize that everything smells better. You realize your sense of smell is returning and improving in ways you didn't know you had lost. It is so wonderful to smell a wonderful clean day after the rain has washed everything clean. You notice the smell of the most delicate flower. Everything is wonderful. Suddenly you enjoy food again, and you find you enjoy foods you had never thought you would. Good for you food groups that now taste so wonderful because your sense of smell has improved so greatly. You have learned to drink water and keep yourself hydrated.

Your skin has improved. The impurities of the cigarettes are completely out of your system, and you are looking and feeling so good. Yes, this is such a wonderful decision, and each day gets better and better and better.

Suddenly you can't imagine why you didn't make this decision many years ago. If you had only known how easy it was. You should feel so proud. So proud, because now you are a non-smoker.

You find you can be around people that smoke, and it never makes you have an urge to light a cigarette. You can't imagine that you ever smoked. It seems like such a foreign thing to you now. In fact, if anything, the smell makes you want to get away. You can't imagine why you never noticed the smell before, but you know you don't like the smell now. You want fresh, smoke-free smells and every time you see someone with a cigarette or smell the smoke of a cigarette, it only further encourages you and cements your decision to become a non-smoker. Yes, you are a non-smoker, and you feel such a sense of freedom. Freedom like you've never felt before.

A freshness, a fresh start on life. Your lungs immediately start repairing themselves, and with each passing year, the tissue of your lungs continues to regenerate until they are the rich pink healthy color they are supposed to be. You can walk up stairs, you can ride a bike, you can run. You can do anything you want now because you no longer run out of breath. You automatically are more active because you feel so much better. You are SOOOO much better because you ARE a non-smoker.

Transition to Motherhood By Kate Nethercott Wilson, CHT

I want to imagine or feel yourself in a beautiful garden on a perfect weatherday. Take a moment to explore the garden, getting a sense of what is around you...breathing in the scent of the flowers and trees, feeling the soft grass under your feet. You feel safe and at peace in this space. It's as if you've been here many times before. It is in this relaxed place you are going to focus on your thoughts and feelings about your transition to motherhood. Acknowledge and embrace who you have been up to the present and honor this new stage in your life as you accept and embrace motherhood.

As you walk around the garden feeling peaceful and safe, I want you to imagine or sense yourself coming across a large mirror. See or just get a sense of what it looks like, its color and size. As you stand in front of the mirror, you notice your reflection looking back at you. As you look at your reflection, just pay attention to any thoughts and feelings that you may have about your life right now as you make the transition to motherhood.

Perhaps your baby's birth didn't go as you had planned....you may be feeling anxious or uncertain about your ability to care for your baby, you may be tired and overwhelmed, sad one minute and joyful the next, or perhaps you are feeling none of these things at all. However you are feeling, take a moment just to acknowledge and accept all of your feelingsand thoughts about motherhood......

The transition to motherhood can be one of the most joyful and challengingtimes for women. It is normal for you to experience a range of feelings and emotions. There is no one right way to feel. Even though you may have friends and family who are mothers, no one else's experience is quite like yours. You are special and unique. In this transition to motherhood, it is important that you accept and acknowledge all of your feelings. There is noone right way to feel or be.

Good....now as you look in the mirror, staying relaxed and calm, take some time to really honor and acknowledge all that you are.....acknowledge all ofyour inner strengths, talents and courage that have brought you to this place in your life today. Really look at yourself....... You successfully navigated your pregnancy, and you have a beautiful healthy baby in your life. Isn't it amazing the way your body supported the growth of your baby? Isn't it amazing how you just did it all and how your life can change in one small moment as your baby enters the world? Thank your body, thank your mind, and thank your spirit for supporting you so well through this transition.

Good...now take a deep breath and allow each and every cell of your body to feel at peace with where you are right now. No matter how your birth was or how you may be feeling, the truth is you have done such an amazing job to bring your new baby into the world. Now, look in the mirror again and this time, see yourself smiling, flowing with the day, handling the transition to motherhood with skill and ease. Beautiful.......

Now feeling completely relaxed and at peace, take some time now just to enjoy your garden. You may wish to walk around and explore, or you may wish to simply lie down and relax. Whatever you choose to do, just let go of control. You are relaxed and open to new ideas and ways of being.

You now release and let go of any and all worries you may have about your ability to take care of your baby. Let go of feelings of fear, doubt and anxiety. Remember that other people's opinions of you and your mothering skills have no influence upon you. You listen to your intuition and acknowledge all your feelings; however, your inner confidence is unwavering. You are truly empowered to make all of the right choices for you and your baby, easily and comfortably. You trust that you already know what is best for you and your baby. Your baby is like no other, and you are meant to be together.

At this special and important time in your life, you chose to surround yourself with nurturing and supportive people. At the same time, you trust that you know what is best for you and your baby. If you are feeling uncertain or overwhelmed, you simply take a deep breath, close your eyes and go within. You listen to your intuition and know that you already have all the knowledge and wisdom that you need to be the perfect mother for your baby. With each day that passes, you feel your inner mother wisdom grow stronger as you get to know your baby and this new aspect of yourself and your life.

You are patient and gentle with yourself and your body. Your body has gone through amazing changes to bring your baby into the world. These changes happen gradually over the space of 9 months, and you accept that it will take time for your body to adapt once again to this new stage in your life. Honor your body and the changes it has gone through to bring your baby into the world. Take the time to move and nurture your body each day and support yourself with healthy, nourishing food.

Even though you may be busy balancing many things in your life, while you adapt to your new role as a mother, you remain relaxed and calm. With each passing day, you feel better and better, and you experience more peace and joy, knowing you are exactly where you need to be and you have everything you need within you to handle all that life and motherhood brings. It is possible to be yourself and to have your needs met as you raise and nurture your baby. You are worthy of help and support, and you are worthy of a rich and fulfilling life that includes being a mother.

Now you are completely calm and at peace with being a mother. You are exactly where you are supposed to be. This is the perfect time for you to be a mother and the perfect baby for you. You have all of the tools, wisdom and knowledge within you to provide for this baby and to care for yourself as you transition to motherhood.

As you move forward in each day as a mother, you will continue to feel this peace. Your thoughts and feelings about motherhood are completely positive and peaceful.

Compulsive Eating While Watching TV Script
By Garvin De Shazier, CHT

As I slowly breathe in one more large, cleansing breath ... then slowly, gently exhale ... letting every last trace of tension flow easily out of my body and away from me ... I am now reaching the deepest level of relaxation ... It feels so very good, so warm and comfortable, to just rest in this place ... I now see that I am worthy of so much more than the shallow and self-destructive behavior of mindlessly eating my life away in front of the TV ... I choose to separate eating from watching TV, so I can become more conscious of both ... I now limit my TV watching to four hours a week, at most ... And, when I eat, I remain free of the distraction of TV, so that I can taste each bite ... knowing that I am also limiting my intake of food to just what I need to maintain good health.

Choosing this new, healthy lifestyle is opening the path to richer, higher pleasures for me ... including the absence of pain, fun physical activities, feeling more attractive and confident, better sex, longer life, greater vitality, freedom of movement and much, much more.

I eat consciously, remaining aware of what my body needs to create and maintain optimum health ... I now 'Eat to live' rather than 'Live to eat.'

I choose to go to bed at a sensible time each night, so I can make sure I get a good night's sleep, and awake feeling refreshed and ready for an early start in the morning ... I choose to get an early start on my work in the morning ... I only accept the tasks I can comfortably complete in a reasonable time ... I choose to leave work by 5:30 every evening ... I come home for a healthy and pleasant dinner with my wife as we talk and listen to music ... I fully accept the responsibility for taking care of myself.

As an adult, I can see that what was truly meaningful to me in the memory of my childhood was my mother's expression of love for me ... I know she would want me to choose health now instead of staying stuck in nostalgia.

... I responsibly reward myself by feeling the love of my family, who support me in making these choices ... I see my wife's face and my children's faces, beaming with pride at how fit and healthy I am ... at how well I'm doing with these choices.

I choose to replace distraction with awareness ... to truly live my life and fully experience each precious moment ... This includes eating responsibly and limiting my TV time.

My standard is no longer what is easy, but rather, what is best ... I now claim a quality of life based on conscious, empowered choices!

I keep food closed up in the pantry, away from where I sit at night ... Every time I touch the handle of the pantry door, I remember that I will take only what my body needs for this new lifestyle I have chosen ... I have also installed a reading light over my chair, and I keep a stack of good books that I am reading where the food used to be ... Whenever I see the books, I want to turn off the TV and enjoy my reading.

I recognize the power of habits in my life, for either good or bad ... so I am choosing to replace the old habit of watching TV with reading, learning, listening to music and fun activities.

I now spend my evenings communicating with my wife, enjoying her companionship and conversation ... As we both become more physically fit, we find more fun activities we like to do together.

I am so pleased with these choices ... I know this is how I now live ... I feel so confident and self-assured in the fitness and health I am achieving ... I feel so loved by my family and my friends ... I am now ready to awaken, remembering every word I've heard and accepting these new choices as an unbreakable commitment to myself and all the people I love ... as I count to five, breathing in and out once for each number ...one, now beginning to become aware of the room around me ... two, noticing my breathing ... three, feeling the health and vitality flow through every part of my body ... four, feeling my eyelids open ... and five, come back into full consciousness and feeling completely energized!

The Ultimate Goal Achievement Script
By Steve Haight, CHT

Now let your mind imagine that it is like a missile! Your mind is like a Missile! You write down your goals in every major area of your life, from greatest to least. Your mind locks onto your goal target and will stay locked until it is reached and Super-Sonic speeds! Once the target is reached, you move on to the next target easily and effortlessly!

Your goals make you feel: Joy and Happiness! Enthusiasm and Eagerness! With Total Certainty of Achievement!

You write goals in every major area of life: Intellectual goals, Emotional goals, Activity goals, Physical goals, Spiritual Goals, Financial goals, Relationship goals, Health and Fitness goals. Your mind is like a missile!

You write your goals down in a positive way that makes you feel Joy and Happiness! ... Enthusiasm and Eagerness! With Total Certainty of Achievement! When you feel all of these emotions, you will know that youare on Target!

Your mind is like a missile! You imagine every aspect of your goal: Imagine seeing.... touching, feeling your goal. Imagine moving... hearing... smelling. And tasting your goal. Imagine all the good feelings. Imagine all the good emotions! Imagine the good thoughts, imagine intuiting.

Your mind is like a missile! It scans and seeks out all the necessary data to make decisions in the fastest, the smartest, the easiest, the wisest, a most effortless way to the target that makes you feel: Joy and Happiness! .... Enthusiasm and Eagerness!

With Total Certainty of Achievement! You can relax now because you know that you achieve ALL your goals now easily, effortlessly, efficiently, at Super-Sonic speeds. Andyou Love it! Everyone is amazed, including YOU!

Your mind is like a missile! Your mind can correct course in nano-seconds if necessary to remain locked on target, and because of this, no obstacle, whether internal or external, can stand in your way now! Your mind just simply finds the best and safest path around the obstacles and heads straight to the target easily and effortlessly with Super-Sonic speed!

You can relax now because <u>you know</u> that you achieve ALL your goals now easily, effortlessly, efficiently, at Super-Sonic speeds. And you Love it! Everyone is amazed, <u>including YOU!</u>

Weight Loss I
By Mary Stoner, CHT

Being in this relaxed state that you are now in, you may be hearing every word that I say…or you may only be hearing bits and pieces. As your mind strays back and forth…here…and there…it doesn't matter whether you're listening to me as I speak or not…all you need to do is relax…

From now on, you will eat only healthy meals, not becoming hungry in between meals…You'll not want to overeat or stuff yourself because you'll feel so much healthier, so much happier, and much more vigorous without an uncomfortable, overfilled stomach. You will eat until you are satisfied and not until you are stuffed…You will best accomplish this by eating slowly.

When you snack, you will only eat healthy items. Candy, sweets, crunchy snacks, and foods filled with preservatives become more unappealing to you as you realize eating healthy is not only better for you…eating healthy foods also taste better.

You will no longer let your emotions take over and affect the physical thoughts about yourself. You are an amazingly beautiful person. You love yourself, every curve, every bump, and every wave. People come in all different shapes and sizes, and that's ok, you know. When you look into the mirror, you see an amazing, confident, attractive and genuine joyous person.

When you wake up in the morning, you feel refreshed and energetic. Throughout the day, you feel as if nothing can stop you because the energy just keeps flowing! You are able to keep up with your daily tasks feeling at ease. Work and play, it doesn't matter because you are strong, confident and capable of achieving all that you set your mind to.

Working out is something that you look forward to doing every day. You are confident in walking, running, swimming, and hiking, whatever active activity you like, because you feel extremely accomplished after every workout session.

You will find that you are drinking water more than you ever have before…water will be there to help you lose weight and to remain healthy. With each meal and through every workout, you will drink a full glass of water because you know that it will continue to hydrate your body and help speed up your metabolism leading to more weight loss.

You'll not lose weight so quickly that it will harm your health, but you will lose weight in a steady constant manner…and with your new lighter figure, you'll find that no matter where you are physically, you are a beautiful, strong, confident, and capable person.

Weight loss II Increased Metabolism
By Leslie Freidlander, CHT

Now you are sitting there relaxing…. Take a deep breath and exhale…. Take a second breath and exhale when you take the next breath as you exhale, go deeper… deeper and deeper… letting your body relax totally. Now as you relax your body … Think about relaxing your whole body…. Letting go of any tense…. Letting go of any stress…..letting of any worries. You are relaxing and letting go of all those feelings. You are feeling free of all negative feelings. Now see yourself walking on a beautiful sandy beach….. feel the warm sand underneath your feet and even in between your toes….feel the warm sunlight touching your face….hear the water hitting the rocks and coming up on the sand… touching your feet. Now relax deeper….deeper and even deeper, letting go. You are getting healthier and healthier …. You are feeling good and healthy. Now, as you are on the beach… your metabolism begins to work better and faster, making you healthier and thinner. You are thinking of only eating better and healthier food.... You are making better chooses... eating healthier. You are not snaking... You are not drinking or eating sweets. In place of them, you are eating healthy things. You are drinking fresh cool water, and it tastes good to you...you crave water all the time. Now see yourself slim and healthy in every way...you see yourself getting thinner and thinner... healthier and healthier. Now you will look into a mirror and see yourself thin.... Beautiful...and... healthy...

Weight Loss III Physical Health By Karen L Chaney, CHT

As you drift down deeper and deeper, imagine yourself experiencing all the wonderful feelings of losing weight. You become healthier and healthier in your food choices and image. You feel your self-esteem increase, and exercise becomes easier and easier. You imagine the healthy you hydrated with skin that glows, and others see this too.

As you become healthier, you can feel your self-esteem increase…growing stronger and stronger. Isn't it wonderful to know that you are capable of increasing your self-esteem? Many people, Karen, have strong, healthy self-esteem, and you will too. Maybe you will notice your confidence rise when you are at the office or when you are home, or when you are at the store.

As you become healthier and your confidence grows, you start to notice the foods you eat. You desire the foods that you know are nutritious. Imagine you are holding the biggest apple you have ever seen. Notice the stem, the roundness of the skin, the color, and its weight. It feels heavy in hand, and you know when you bite into it, it's just the right amount of sweetness for you. Now imagine taking a bite from the apple, hear it and feel the wonderful sensation of the goodness of that apple as it fills your entire body, taking nutrients to every part from your toes up through your body to your head.

As your body becomes stronger and stronger using all the nutrients from the healthy foods you eat, you notice that you have the self-control to continue to make good choices. When you drive by your favorite fast-food restaurant, you know you can choose to eat those things, and as you are ready, they will become less and less appealing as you want the apple and other foods that make your body feel so energized and healthy.

And as you are more and more energized, you may begin to feel restless. It is ok to feel restless. Now imagine you are outside on a nice, easy dirt path. You hear the birds chirping and feel the wind as it gently brushes your face. Now turn your face into the sun and feel the rays touching your skin as you begin to walk. You may notice the restlessness from before is becoming less and less. As you breathe the air deeply into your lungs, you begin to walk and feel the restlessness decrease. Walking feels good, and you feel the blood carrying the healthy nutrients through the body.

When you are ready, you will stop walking and look down at your body. You will sense it is physically getting smaller as your self-esteem and control are growing stronger. As you walk back along the path, enjoy the feeling of your body working perfectly and in harmony with your life. In the distance is a small light, and it grows bigger as you walk toward it. As you get closer, you realize it's not light but the light that is coming from you as you see your perfect self as others see you.

Weight Loss IV
By Rita Lake, CHT

You are very relaxed ... feeling very calm.

Now that you've made the decision to lose weight, I want you to visualize how you will look when you reach your goal weight... See yourself in a full-length mirror and notice how slender your face and neck are...how narrow your waist is...how flat your stomach is... You will look great, won't you?

You can lose this weight at a reasonable... healthy pace. Every day is progress towards your goal... you are strong and successful. You won't skip meals anymore...you will crave healthy foods...vegetables ....chicken... fish.... see yourself leaving food behind on your plate...you no longer snack at night... when you feel the desire to eat something unhealthy you will get a bottle of water and drink it very slowly.

As clothes become too large for you, I want you to put them in a bag and donate them to charity...you don't need them anymore...see yourself going to the store... having fun shopping for new clothes to fit your new figure. You deserve it... you earned it.

Weight Loss, Reflection
By Tibbeth Jordan, CHT

As you reach the bottom of the stairs, you see a door to the right.

Opening the door, you enter into a beautiful room. At the far side of the room, French doors bring a soft ocean breeze whirling around you. Near the open doors, an ornate mirror catches your eye. Instantly, you find yourself drawn towards this mirror. You step before the mirror, reflecting every angle. In the mirror, you see the reflection of the perfect you: the correct size and weight you want to be. You see yourself in all the different angles, with all the curves in all right places. Your clothes fit perfectly against your body. Your posture is that of someone with confidence. That of someone that can handle any situation. Realizing that you have all the strength and abilities to reach any goals that you set. As you gaze into the true beauty of your reflection, you speak to yourself with the knowledge of perfect wisdom.

As you breathe in a cleansing breath, you breathe in the desire for health. And as you exhale slowly, you are releasing the desire for fatty foods and sugar. And you feel the release of desire with every breath. From now on, you will chew your food longer and slower and pull flavor and enjoyment from your food. From now on, you will seek out and eat only healthy foods that serve your purpose and strengthen your body. You will resist items with fats and sugars. You will no longer desire these foods.

You will now find these foods easy to resist. You will always eat fresh fruits and vegetables. You will be conscious to drink lots of water every day and will find imaginative ways to implement exercise daily as a source of enjoyment. From this moment on, your actions, decisions, and choices will be reflective of your new mindset to live a healthy lifestyle. You will be conscious in some way every day to exercise and strengthen your body.

You will only make decisions with foods that serve your body and goalsbest.

As you gaze at the reflection of the perfect you, your whole being celebrates this decision of healthy living and lifestyle. Notice the reflection of the perfect you, reaching out a hand to touch yours. As your hands touch, feel an unconditional source of love from your reflection. And as you feel this unconditional love flow into your heart, know that this love will allow you to find the discipline to now pass on foods that don't serve to nourish your body and healthy lifestyle. Feel the love and conviction to step into this new life of health. A new body that feels strong and alive, healthy, vibrant and supports your new, healthy, active life. And now, step forward as you become your reflection. Feel how wonderful this strong and healthy body feels. Feel this state of perfect health.

Weight Management
By Shirley Dunlap, CHT

You are so relaxed, you're so comfortable, and you feel so good because you have decided it is time to take control of your weight. And you know that when your weight drops, you will feel healthier right away. And with each passing day that you feel healthier, you will want to continue to become healthier, and you will start to exercise. Exercise comes in many forms; it doesn't have to be a formal exercise program. It may become a formal exercise program, but for now, you are just going to notice that you prefer to take the step instead of the elevator whenever you have a choice. You find yourself wondering why anyone would wait for a closer parking space instead of choosing the space that's further away, just to get a few more steps in – in such an easy, effortless, automatic way.

You feel so good, so relaxed. You realize now that you don't have to cover and fill your entire plate with food. You can safely have smaller portions of food. You don't have to deprive yourself. You simply take smaller portions. And it's always okay if you decide you don't have to try some of every foodput in front of you. You feel so good because you think of food now as a fuel for your body, a nice clean fuel that burns clean because it burns calories appropriately when you eat healthy. When you let the food pyramid be your guide to what you eat. You know you should have whole grains and vegetables with protein and smaller portions of carbohydrates. You are not hooked on any particular food group, and you do not deprive yourself of a food group either. You do not crave carbs. You do not crave sweets. You are feeling so good and so healthy.

You've realized a healthy breakfast is an excellent way to start the day. It gives you the energy you need to think clearly and start the day with healthy energy. Energy that is so healthy. Spending time thinking of whenyou can have your next meal is no longer your main thought. In fact, it's hardly ever a thought. You only eat when you're hungry. You know your next meal is appropriate. A healthy lunch is when you're body wants some more energy, healthy proteins and carbohydrates to complete your day. It feels so good to eat healthy. It tastes so good. Your taste buds have adapted so that when you eat, you automatically make better choices. It's okay if you don't eat everything. It's perfectly okay to leave food on your plate. You eat slowly and digest your food, and your body tells your brain when you are full. At that time, you know you have had enough food, and it's time to stop. It doesn't matter how much food is left on the plate. You might now consider the garbage disposal your best friend, that wonderful friend that you love sharing a meal with. You never hesitate to share some of your food with your disposal. This feels so good to know there are no rules that say you have to clean everything off your plate. You do not have to eat everything on your plate. Maybe you'll wrap up half of the food that was on your plate. One lunch has now become two lunches, enough for the next day. Leftovers taste so good. And now you notice more cash in your pocket ... you're spending half as much on food during the workday as you used to. You have learned to eat smaller portions. It feels so good. You feel so good.

You're last meal of the day proportional also. Dinner doesn't have to be the biggest meal of the day. It's okay if it's a smaller meal. And you have now decided to eat dinner a minimum of three hours before bedtime. Now you sleep better. Your stomach is settled. You do not go to bed hungry. You wake ready for a healthy breakfast to start the day. You find the pounds are melting off. You are not deprived, and you feel better and healthier with each passing day. Every day is a pleasure, and the foods you eat are now a pleasure. You eat healthy, so each bite you take isn't paired with a feeling of guilt. It's paired with knowing you are giving your body the proper fuel it needs in the proper portions, and you feel so good, so healthy, so attractive. You have so much energy. Everything you do is now more enjoyable. Your clothes fit better. You feel so good. Everyone notices how good you look. Compliments flow freely and encourage you even more to continue down this road of healthy eating.

Weight Release
By Kim Balzan, CHT

I want you to take a deeeeep breath…you are so relaxed. Every time I say the word **NOW,** you will find yourself going deeper into relaxation. It feels soo good to just relax and imagine your body looking and feeling wonderful.

You are always choosing healthier foods **now**. You love the colorful fruits and vegetables. They taste so good to you **now**. You are feeling lighter, releasing any excess weight, that's right, the weight has just started to fall off…in the past, you went from diet to diet, but **now** things are different, things are better its almost as if eating healthy just comes so natural to you….

You are feeling so much lighter and more comfortable in your clothes. They are just fitting better…more comfortable…you're feeling more confident… It's so good to feel confident about your body…**Now** when you see your reflection, that's exactly what it is… a reflection …of you looking and feeling wonderful. **Now** it's easy to imagine your body looking the way you want it to.... because it really is... it's happening this time you are releasing the weight you no longer need... **now** you say to yourself. I am inches away from perfection... just inches away.... you are always smiling knowing that health is yours **now**, you are important to you.... you take care of you **now**... you are amazed at how your habits have changed, **now** you are eating a wonderful breakfast in the morning, in the past, you may not have eaten breakfast at all.... but it's different **now**...You are important .... and it shows... no more skipping meals for you....your loving the way you look and feel... it's soo good to feel love towards your body now... you take pride in taking care of yourself, and it shows... Preparing meals or snacks is easy **now**... you enjoy it **now**..... and you are choosing foods that are satisfying... filling ...balanced meals.... balanced life .... That's you.... everything is balanced ... even your thoughts ...

You are finding that releasing weight comes soo easy.... soo easy this time...its effortless... your choices are paying off... you're loving life... and it feeeeeels good.... your body feels good... you're even adding movement .... it feels good to move your body **now** because it's lighter ...it's easier... effortless ... it's better **now**.... and getting better every day.... you know it... you feel it ... you see it... you love to look at your body **now**... the progress that you are making... releasing weight has given you back you're confidence.. you are excited about your life, and it feels good...

Writing a Best Seller
By Connie Brown, CHT

Take a few more deep breaths... That's good ...You are imagining a sunny shack on a beach with a quiet, cozy writing nook. You are envisioning a window seat with orangey peach and pale blue pillows, a simple table, anda small green teacup. In the middle of the single room's wooden floor wouldbe one of those colorful, tightly-coiled rugs made of leftover cloth. Giant leaflithographs framed on the walls, a single bookshelf with all of your favorites, and a wood stove with brass feet that look like lion feet. Handfuls of seashells here and there, driftwood. Ahhh. You feeeeel soooo wonderful. I wonder what you would write about? You see a computer that is just calling for you to create a best seller. You start typing... the words just flow out of you... You take a deep breath and relax... you are halfway through your story... with each stroke of the keys, you become more and more confident with your work as a best seller... you are coming to the end of your book... you see the computer screen very clear... as you type... The End. You are pleased in every way... so excited to get your bestseller published. It is time to come back now… feeling better than before… taking your time to come back to a waking state… counting from 1-4

1… Feeling better than before 2… Feeling so creative

3… Eyes starting to open And

4… Wide awake, feeling wonderful in every way.

Awakening I
By Kyra Schaefer, CHI

You will take these suggestions beyond today, into tomorrow and further into the future.

In a moment, I will begin counting from 1 to 5. When I reach the number 5, you will wake feeling better than ever.

1... Coming back into the room.

2... Beginning to feel your fingers and toes, arms and legs, face and head.

3... Taking a few good deep breaths, waking up from the inside out.

4... Feeling better and better from the tips of your toes to the top of your head.

5... Waking up, eyes open, feeling great.

Awakening II
By Kyra Schaefer, CHI

That's right, now beginning the process of coming back into the room. In a moment, I am going to beginning counting from 5 down to 1. When I reach number 1, I will snap my fingers, and you will come fully back to waking consciousness.

5… Coming back more and more.

4… Allowing yourself to feel your body more and more.

3… Taking a few deep breaths, letting yourself come back easily.

2… Fully feeling your body, completely in the room.

And 1 (snap fingers) all the way back wide awake.

Awakening III
By Kyra Schaefer, CHI

As you continue to relax, I will invite your subconscious mind to process all the information being given to it. I will quiet down, and when I speak again, all those processes will be complete. (wait approx. 1 minute or more) That's right…

Now I will begin to count from 1 to 5. When I reach the number 5, you will come all the way back to waking consciousness.

1… Feeling more and more awake.

2… Enjoying the feeling of coming back into the room.

3… Letting yourself take a couple deep breaths.

4… Waking more and more.

And finally 5…All the way back, eyes open, wide awake.

www.ingramcontent.com/pod-product-compliance
Lightning Source LLC
Chambersburg PA
CBHW070850050426
42453CB00012B/2127